America's Middle Schools in the New Century
Status and Progress

National Middle School Association is dedicated to improving the educational experiences of young adolescents by providing vision, knowledge, and resources to all who serve them in order to develop healthy, productive, and ethical citizens.

AMERICA'S MIDDLE SCHOOLS IN THE NEW CENTURY

STATUS AND PROGRESS

C. Kenneth McEwin

Thomas S. Dickinson

Doris M. Jenkins

National Middle School Association
Westerville, Ohio

National Middle School Association
4151 Executive Parkway, Suite 300
Westerville, Ohio 43081
1-800-528-NMSA
www.nmsa.org

Copyright© 2003 by National Middle School Association.

All rights reserved. No part of this publication may be reproduced or transmitted in any form or by any means, electronic or mechanical, without permission in writing from the publisher except in the case of brief quotations embodied in reviews or articles.

The materials presented herein are the expressions of the authors and do not necessarily represent the policies of NMSA.

NMSA is a registered servicemark of National Middle School Association.
Printed in the United States of America

Sue Swaim, Executive Director
Jeff Ward, Associate Executive Director
Edward Brazee, Editor, Professional Publications
John Lounsbury, Consulting Editor, Professional Publications
Mary Mitchell, Designer, Editorial Assistant
Marcia Meade-Hurst, Senior Publications Representative
Sara Levengood, Production Manager

Library of Congress Cataloging in Publication Data
McEwin, C. Kenneth
    America's middle schools in the new century: status and progress/C. Kenneth McEwin
    Thomas S. Dickinson, Doris M. Jenkins
        p. cm.
    Includes bibliographical references.
    ISBN: 1-56090-136-5 (pbk.)
      1. Middle schools--United States--Evaluation. 2. Middle schools--United
    States--Statistics. I. Dickinson, Thomas S. II. Jenkins, doris M., (date) -III. Title.

LB1623.5.M33 2003
373.236'0973--dc21   2003044159

To our children's children

Sarah Kathleen Lyons
Holly Edith Lyons

Thomas Wilson Jardine

Courtney Ann Parker
Roberto Vicente Arza
Rhianna Kelly Jenkins
Cody Dalton Jenkins
Kylie Jenna Jenkins
Keanan Anthony Jenkins
Landon James Jenkins

About the Authors

C. Kenneth McEwin is Professor of Curriculum and Instruction at Appalachian State University, Boone, North Carolina. He is an author, researcher, consultant, charter member and past-president of National Middle School Association, and recipient of the John H. Lounsbury Distinguished Service Award.

Thomas S. Dickinson is Professor of Education, DePauw University, Greencastle, Indiana. A former editor of *Middle School Journal,* he is a prolific author of articles, books, research reports, and other professional publications, many dealing with teacher education. Dr. Dickinson has also served in a variety of leadership positions.

Doris M. Jenkins is Professor of Curriculum and Instruction and Associate Dean of the Reich College of Education, Appalachian State University, Boone, North Carolina. Active in middle level education for many years, she has authored numerous professional publications.

Gratitude to Respondents

The authors wish to extend their deep gratitude to the principals and other professional personnel at the 746 middle level schools who took time from their busy schedules to respond to this comprehensive survey. We hope that the resulting information will prove useful to them and their colleagues across the nation. We also express our thanks to the staff at National Middle School Association and the College of Education at Appalachian State University, Boone, North Carolina, for their valuable assistance and support. As always, John H. Lounsbury and his excellent editing skills have greatly improved the quality of this report. We are privileged to know him as a mentor and friend.

Table of Contents

Lists of Tables and Figures — p. ix

Foreword, *John H. Lounsbury* — p. xi

Part I. Introduction — p. 1
    Background Information
    The 1968, 1988, and 1993 Studies
    The 2001 Study

Part II. Middle School Programs and Practices — p. 9
    School Enrollment
    Team Organization
    Remedial Instruction Arrangements
    Scheduling Plans
    Time Allotted for Core Instruction
    Other Required Subjects
    Elective Subjects Offered
    Interest Class/Mini-Course Programs
    Teacher-Based Guidance (Advisory) Programs
    Interschool Sports
    Interdisciplinary Instruction
    Use of Selected Instructional Strategies
    Instructional Grouping Practices
    Student Progress Reports
    Faculty
    High Stakes Testing

Part III. Conclusions and Recommendations — p. 41
    Grade Organization Trends
    School Size
    Team Organization
    Remedial Instruction Arrangements
    Scheduling Plans
    Time Allocated for Core Instruction
    Required Non-Core Subjects
    Elective Subjects

    Interest Class/Mini-Course Programs
    Teacher-Based Guidance (Advisory) Programs
    Interschool Sports Programs
    Interdisciplinary Instruction and Instructional Strategies
    Instructional Grouping Practices
    Student Progress Reports
    Faculty
    High Stakes Testing
    Concluding Statements

References — p. 68

LIST OF TABLES

TABLE

1. Number of Middle Schools of Various Grade Organizations: 1970, 1986, 1992, 1999, and 2001 6
2. Number and Percent of Surveys Mailed and Returned 6
3. Number and Percent of Grade Organization Patterns of Responding Schools 6
4. Number of Responses by State 7
5. Number and Percent of Responses by Community Type 7
6. Number and Percent of Enrollments of Schools 11
7. Percent of Enrollments of Schools: 1968, 1988, 1993, and 2001 12
8. Percent of Enrollments of Schools by Community Type 12
9. Percent of Schools Utilizing Selected Team Sizes by Grade Level 14
10. Percent of Common Planning Periods Per Week 15
11. Percent of Selection Methods for Team Leaders: 1993 and 2001 16
12. Percent of Scheduling Plans Utilized by Schools: 1993 and 2001 17
13. Percent of Schools Utilizing Selected Number of Daily Uniform Periods 17
14. Percent of Schools Offering Required and Elective Subjects: 2001 20
15. Percent of Schools Offering Required and Elective Subjects: 1993 21
16. Percent of Schools With Mini-Course Programs: 1993 and 2001 25
17. Percent of Schools Utilizing Selected Mini-Course Themes 25
18. Percent of Minutes Advisory Scheduled: 1988, 1993, and 2001 26
19. Percent of Frequency of Advisory Meetings: 1988, 1993, and 2001 27
20. Percent of Schools Offering Selected Interschool Sports Programs for Boys: 1993 and 2001 28
21. Percent of Schools Offering Selected Interschool Sports Programs for Girls: 1993 and 2000 30
22. Number and Percent of Changes in Interschool Sports Programs 30
23. Percent of Interdisciplinary Instruction: 1993 and 2001 31
24. Percent of Schools Utilizing Selected Types of Instructional Strategies: 1993 and 2001 32
25. Percent of Ability Grouping/Tracking Practices: 1993 and 2001 34
26. Percent of Schools Ability Grouping/Tracking in Selected Subjects 34
27. Percent of Schools Utilizing Selected Methods of Reporting Pupil Progress: 1968, 1988, 1993, and 2001 36
28. Percent of Teachers With Specialized Middle Level Teacher Preparation: 1988, 1993, and 2001 36

29. Percent of Teachers Wishing to Leave the Middle Level:
   1993 and 2001 _____ 38
30. Percent of Schools Reporting Varying Levels of Impact of High Stakes
   Testing on Selected Middle School Components _____ 39
31. Percent of Schools Reporting Varying Levels of High Stakes Testing
   on the Use of Time _____ 39

LIST OF FIGURES

FIGURE
1. Percent of Middle Schools Using Team Organization:
   1988, 1993, and 2001 _____ 14
2. Percent of Special Remedial Arrangements: 1993 and 2001 _____ 16
3. Mean Instructional Minutes Per Day in Core Subjects _____ 19
4. Percent of Most Frequently Required Non-Core
   Seventh Grade Courses _____ 22
5. Percent of Most Frequently Offered Seventh Grade Elective Courses ____ 24
6. Percent of Schools With Advisory Programs: 1988, 1993, and 2001 ____ 26
7. Percent of Middle Schools With Interschool Sports Programs:
   1968, 1988, 1993, and 2001 _____ 28
8. Percent of Most Frequently Offered Seventh Grade Girls' and Boys'
   Interschool Sports Programs _____ 29
9. Percent of Schools Utilizing Cooperative Learning
   on a Regular Basis: 1993 and 2001 _____ 33
10. Percent of Teachers With Specialized Middle Level
    Teacher Preparation: 1988, 1993, and 2000 _____ 37

Foreword

If we could first know where we are and whither we are tending, we could better judge what to do and how to do it. — Abraham Lincoln

Add the phrase, "where we came from" and this statement by Lincoln would fit perfectly as a justification for and an introduction to this new status study. Knowing where we are now – the present, knowing where we came from – the past, and knowing what the trends are provide a solid basis for charting the course of middle level education in the 21st century.

The turn of the century may be something of a watershed period for middle level education. The euphoria that accompanied the early growth in the 70s and 80s has subsided somewhat. The harsh realities that surround making "second level" changes have become all too apparent. The pervasive holding power of institutionalized schooling is confronted daily. The test-based accountability movement has almost brought to a halt many middle school practices. Yet persistence still characterizes middle level educators and the work of National Middle School Association. Optimism, though tempered, still abounds; but just where are we?

It is time to take stock, to contemplate the reality of our present status, to confirm progress where it exists, and to accept the lack of it where that is the case. We have not had the data needed to consider the impact of accountability by SAT scores, the introduction of technology, and the budget cuts that have characterized recent years. We sense progress in some areas, but losses in others. We have glowing reports from a number of schools, but reports of retrenchment from others. Now this major study has provided much needed information. It is the most comprehensive study conducted on the state of middle level schooling since its predecessor in 1993. It paints a fairly detailed picture of just where we are in this major educational movement. The extent of the random sample makes it possible to generalize for the total population. The data are broken down in many ways so that conclusions can be drawn. For example, the data permit us to compare interschool sports programs offered for boys with those offered for girls. To grasp all the information available in this report one needs not only to read the text carefully but also examine the tables and consider the conclusions and recommendations.

What makes this report unique and of even more value is its ability to provide perspective, to make comparisons with the status of middle schools in 1968, 1988, and 1993. The instrument that was used to gather data included items from the earlier studies as well as many new items.

Armed with the details provided by this study, educators can make more informed decisions about next steps. And as the data make clear, there are many, large next steps that need to be taken. Progress is evident, yet painfully slow. Considering the clarion call for school reform that has been heard on nearly every hand and the validity of the middle school concept increasingly supported by research, educators need to use these data to make informed decisions as new improvement initiatives are planned.

One final note – as we read these objectively stated statistics and figures and contemplate the significance of a particular percentage gain or the little variance between the numbers from earlier years, it is well to remember that behind these numbers are classroom teachers, principals, other educators, and students. The yeomen service of these individuals has made possible the success of middle level education, a story unparalleled in American education. While we might hope for greater gain, we must not fail to recognize the extraordinary commitment to young adolescents exhibited by thousands of today's educators. When another study is done sometime after another decade has passed, and the results are compared with the present results, I predict gains will be recorded that reflect the continuing vitality of middle level education and the work of these pioneer educators.

John H. Lounsbury
March 2003

Part I

Introduction

Background Information, 3
The 1968, 1988, and 1993 Studies, 4
The 2001 Study, 4

Part I

Introduction

Background Information

American education experienced a major reorganization in the first half of the 20th century. Perhaps the major part of this reorganization was moving from a two-tier elementary and high school system to a three-tier plan consisting of elementary, middle level, and senior high school. The new tier of this reorganization initially was the junior high school. These schools, typically including grades seven through nine, became so popular that by 1960 approximately four of every five high school graduates had attended elementary, junior high, and senior high school. However, the number of junior high schools decreased from more than 6,000 at the peak of their popularity to 4,711 by 1970 (Alexander & McEwin, 1989) as the middle school, usually of grades six through eight, took hold. Junior high schools continued to decline in popularity during the last half of the century with only 632 remaining in the nation by 2001.

The reasons for the emergence of middle schools and the decreasing popularity of junior high schools are well documented in the middle school literature and are not discussed here. It is generally agreed, however, that by most measures junior high schools failed to reach their full potential and too frequently became miniature versions of the senior high school. The decline in the popularity of junior high schools was paralleled by the emergence of a rapid growth of middle schools with the number of these schools reaching 13,512 by 2001 (Market Data Retrieval, 2001). Proposed and supported by early leaders such as William M. Alexander, Donald H. Eichhorn, John H. Lounsbury, and Gordon F. Vars, the new middle school was designed to better reflect the developmental and academic needs of young adolescents. The major components of the middle school have remained largely intact throughout the last three decades of the 20th century and into the beginning of the 21st century. These components are described in detail in current middle school literature and are not discussed here (e.g., Dickinson, 2001; Erb, 2001a; George & Alexander, 2003; National Middle School Association, 1995). However, it should be understood that the current study includes the programs and practices that represent the major tenets of the contemporary middle school proposed by the founders of the middle school and implemented in the nation's middle schools.

The 1968, 1988, and 1993 Studies

The 1968 study referenced throughout this report was the first national comprehensive study of middle schools. Results of this landmark study, conducted by William M. Alexander (1968) during the 1967-68 school year, are used throughout this report as benchmark data from which to gain a historical perspective regarding the progress, and lack thereof, made by the nation's middle schools in the intervening years. The definition of middle schools used in the 1968 study was "a school having at least three grades and not more than five grades, and including at least grades six and seven" (Alexander, 1968, p. 1). After determining that there were 1,101 schools meeting this definition, a 10% random stratified sample was selected. Of these 110 middle schools, 60% were grades 6-8 schools, 27% were grades 5-8 schools, with the remainder having grades 4-8, 5-7, and 4-7. Eighty-three percent (83%) of schools selected responded to the study.

William M. Alexander and C. Kenneth McEwin (1989) conducted the 1988 study utilized in this report during the 1987-88 school year. This national survey was a comprehensive follow-up of the 1968 study. Many survey items from the 1968 study were replicated in the 1988 study. However, some new items were added to provide a more complete picture of middle school programs and practices. An additional change made in the 1988 study was the inclusion of grades 7-9 junior high schools. This was done so that programs and practices in the two kinds of middle level schools could be compared. The return rate on this survey was 56%.

C. Kenneth McEwin, Thomas S. Dickinson, and Doris M. Jenkins conducted the 1993 study used in this report during the 1992-93 school year. Middle level schools with grade organizations of 5-8, 6-8, 7-8, and 7-9 were included in this national survey. One thousand seven hundred ninety-eight schools responded to the survey for an overall return rate of 53%. Items from the 1968 and 1988 studies were included in the survey along with new items that reflected current interests and trends in middle schools. Results from this study offered an updated view of middle level programs and practices and provided a historical perspective over a period of 25 years.

The 2001 Study

The middle school movement has experienced significant success in the years since the first middle schools were established in the 1960s. The number of middle schools has continued to increase significantly while other grade organization plans including the middle grades have rapidly declined in popularity (e.g., K-8, 7-9). Because of the small number of junior high schools remaining at the time of this study (632), data from these rapidly disappearing middle level schools were not collected. The grade organizations of middle schools included in the study are those containing grades 5-8, 6-8, and 7-8. These grade organizations were selected because the vast majority of young adolescents in the nation attend middle schools with one of these grade organizations. The total number of schools with these grade organizations at the time data were collected for the current study was 12,377.

The major purpose of this study of middle schools was to obtain a "snapshot" of current programs and practices in the nation's public middle schools to see just where we are. Data from this study were analyzed using results from comparable studies conducted by the authors and by other researchers over the last three decades (e.g., Alexander, 1968; Alexander & McEwin, 1989; Epstein & MacIver, 1990; McEwin, Dickinson & Jenkins, 1996; Valentine, Clark, Hackmann & Petko, 2002). Because the 1968 Alexander study, the 1988 Alexander & McEwin (1989) study, and the 1993 McEwin, Dickinson, and Jenkins (1996) study are referred to frequently in this report, from this point forward they are referred to as the 1968, the 1988, and the 1993 studies respectively.

Data for the current study were collected during the spring and fall of 2001. As shown in Table 1, the number of middle schools in the nation has increased significantly since the 1968 survey with the grades 6-8 middle school becoming the most popular middle school organizational plan. The number of grades 5-8 middle schools have also increased while grades 7-8 schools have shown a slight decrease (5%). In the spring of 2001, comprehensive surveys were mailed to 1,436 (12%) middle schools and returned by 746 for an overall return rate of 52% (Table 2)

The number and percentage of organizational patterns responding to the survey are presented in Table 3. These response rates closely approximated the percentages of school organizations included in the sample. Table 4 shows the number of responses received from each state. As would be expected, the highest numbers of responses were received from states with the largest number of middle schools (e.g., California, Texas). Respondents were asked to indicate whether the community their school served was rural, urban, or suburban. Forty-one percent (41%) of schools served rural areas, 21% urban areas, and 38% suburban communities (Table 5).

TABLE 1
NUMBER OF MIDDLE SCHOOLS OF VARIOUS GRADE ORGANIZATIONS:
1970, 1986, 1992, 1999, AND 2001

Grade Organization	Number of Schools					Percent of Change
	1970-71	1986-87	1992-93	1999-00	2001-02	
5-8	772	1137	1223	1325	1364	+76
6-8	1662	4326	6155	8290	8690	+422
7-8	2450	2627	2412	2362	2323	-5
Total	4884	8093	9790	11977	12377	+153

TABLE 2
NUMBER AND PERCENT OF SURVEYS MAILED AND RETURNED

Grade Organization	Number of Schools	Number Mailed	Number Returned	Percent of Return
5-8	1,325	159	89	56
6-8	8,290	994	505	51
7-8	2,362	283	152	54
Total	11,977	1,436	746	52

TABLE 3
NUMBER AND PERCENT OF GRADE ORGANIZATION PATTERNS
OF RESPONDING SCHOOLS

Grade Organization	Number	Percent
5-8	89	12
6-8	505	68
7-8	152	20
Total	746	100

TABLE 4
NUMBER AND RESPONSES BY STATE

State	Number	State	Number
Alabama	15	New Hampshire	5
Alaska	2	New Jersey	20
Arizona	9	New Mexico	6
Arkansas	3	New York	33
California	48	North Carolina	31
Colorado	13	North Dakota	2
Connecticut	8	Ohio	42
Delaware	1	Oklahoma	15
Florida	23	Oregon	14
Georgia	18	Pennsylvania	28
Hawaii	1	Rhode Island	5
Idaho	5	South Carolina	16
Illinois	38	South Dakota	8
Indiana	25	Tennessee	18
Iowa	17	Texas	56
Kansas	13	Utah	2
Kentucky	11	Vermont	1
Louisiana	7	Virginia	21
Maine	10	Washington	16
Maryland	11	West Virginia	4
Massachusetts	12	Wisconsin	18
Michigan	26	Wyoming	3
Minnesota	9	Washington, DC	1
Mississippi	6	State Not Provided	20
Missouri	23	Total	746
Montana	7		

TABLE 5
NUMBER AND PERCENT OF RESPONSES BY COMMUNITY TYPE

Community Type	Number	Percent
Rural	294	41
Urban	156	21
Suburban	272	38
Total	722	100

Many of the survey items utilized in this study were also included in those conducted in 1968, 1988, and 1993. However, several new items were added to better reflect current developments in middle school education. Many of the tables and figures include data from the earlier surveys so the reader can gain a more complete perspective on the current status of middle level programs and practices. Some items are new to this survey and therefore no comparative data are available.◆

Part II

Middle School Programs and Practices

School Enrollment, 11

Team Organization, 13

Remedial Instruction Arrangements, 16

Scheduling Plans, 17

Time Allotted for Core Instruction, 18

Other Required Subjects, 19

Elective Subjects Offered, 23

Interest Class/Mini-Course Program, 23

Teacher-Based Guidance (Advisory) Programs, 25

Interschool Sports, 27

Interdisciplinary Instruction, 30

Use of Selected Instructional Strategies, 31

Instructional Grouping Practices, 34

Student Progress Reports, 35

Faculty, 36

High Stakes Testing, 38

Part II

Middle School Programs and Practices

School Enrollment

Respondents were asked to indicate the number of students enrolled in their schools. As shown in Table 6, the most common school size was 601-800 with approximately one-fourth (26%) of schools falling into that range. Twenty-three percent (23%) of schools reported enrollments of between 401 and 600. Therefore, nearly one-half (49%) of middle schools fell into the 401 to 800 range. Although 26% of schools enrolled 801 or more students, many middle schools remain relatively small with 25% housing 400 or fewer students. The smallest school responding to the study had 28 students and the largest 4000. The mean size for all middle schools was 656.

TABLE 6
NUMBER AND PERCENT OF ENROLLMENTS OF SCHOOLS

Enrollment	Number	Percent
1-200	48	7
201-400	131	18
401-600	165	23
601-800	190	26
801-1000	101	14
1001-1200	43	6
1201-1400	18	2
More than 1400	31	4
Totals	727	100

To determine trends in the size (student populations) of middle schools, data from this survey were compared with those of the 1968, 1988, and 1993 studies. The categories of 1-400, 401-800, and more than 800 were used for these comparisons. As shown in Table 7, the percentage of schools enrolling 800 or more students decreased from 30% in 1993 to 26% in 2001. However, the percentages of middle schools within this range were higher than those reported in the 1968 and 1988 studies. The number of schools enrolling from 401 to 800 students had not changed significantly since the 1980s. About one-half of the nation's middle schools fell into this category. The number of middle schools with enrollments of 401 or fewer declined from 39% in 1968 to 22% in 1988, but had increased somewhat since that time (25%).

TABLE 7
PERCENT OF ENROLLMENTS OF SCHOOLS: 1968, 1988, 1993, AND 2001

Range of Enrollment	Percent			
	1968	1988	1993	2001
1-400	39	34	22	25
401-800	45	52	48	49
More than 800	16	14	30	26

Enrollment data were also analyzed by the categories of community type (e.g. rural, urban, suburban) to determine if certain types of communities were more or less likely to have various school enrollment sizes. As might be expected, rural middle schools tended to be smaller than urban and suburban middle schools. One-third of rural middle schools had between 201 and 400 students with an additional 15% enrolling 1-200 students (Table 8). Therefore, 48% of all rural middle schools housed between 1 and 400 students. Not all rural middle schools were small, however, with the remaining 52% having more than 400 students.

TABLE 8
PERCENT OF ENROLLMENTS OF SCHOOLS BY COMMUNITY TYPE

Enrollment	Rural	Urban	Suburban
1-200	15	2	1
201-400	33	8	7
401-600	27	19	21
601-800	16	33	32
801-1000	6	22	19
1001-1200	1	8	9
1201-1400	1	2	4
More than 1400	<1	5	7

By contrast, urban and suburban middle schools were larger and had approximately the same size student populations. For example, the largest percentages (33% and 32%) of schools in both categories reported school populations of between 601 and 800. Only 10% of urban and 8% of suburban middle schools enrolled between 1 and 400 students as compared with 48% of rural middle schools. Fifteen percent (15%) of urban schools and 20% of suburban middle schools reported enrolling more than 1000 students as compared to only 2% of rural middle schools. The large majority of urban and suburban middle schools had enrollments of between 400 and 1000 (74% for urban and 72% for suburban).

In summary, based on responses from the four studies discussed in this report, student enrollments in middle schools increased by the early 1990s.

Status and Progress

Currently, about one-fourth of all middle schools are relatively small (1-400) and about one-fourth relatively large (more than 800). Approximately one-half are of moderate size and enroll between 401 and 800 students. School enrollments have remained relatively constant since the 1993 study with a slight increase in the percentage of small schools (1-400) and a small decrease in the percentages of schools enrolling more than 800 students. Rural middle schools tended to have smaller student populations with few differences in the size of school populations found between urban and suburban middle schools.

Team Organization

One of the most crucial elements of successful middle schools is interdisciplinary team organization. The degree of implementation of this practice is especially important since increasing numbers of studies are showing a correlation between student achievement, as measured by standardized test scores, and the use of team organization and common planning time for teachers (Felner et al., 1997; Felner, Mertens, & Lipsitz, 1996; Flowers, Mertens, & Mulhall, 1999, 2000; McEwin, Greene, & Jenkins, 2001).

The percentage of middle schools in the nation utilizing team organization has increased significantly in recent years (Figure 1). Thirty percent (30%) of middle schools organized teachers into teams in 1988 as compared to 52% in 1993, and 77% in 2001. This represents an increase of 47% since the 1988 study and 25% since the 1993 study. Implementation levels are even higher in states with strong commitments to the middle school plan. For example, in 2000, 98% of middle schools in North Carolina that were recognized as schools of distinction or schools of excellence utilized interdisciplinary team organization (McEwin, Greene & Jenkins, 2001). This recognition is based on results of high stakes tests with 80% or more of students scoring on or above grade level for the first level of recognition and 90% or more for the second level.

Respondents were also asked to provide information about the number of teachers on teams at their schools. The researchers added this item because of numerous inquiries from school representatives where moving to smaller team sizes was under consideration. The most popular team size at all grade levels was four (Table 9). Perhaps this is because interdisciplinary teams typically represent the four core subjects of language arts, mathematics, science, and social studies. The next most popular team size at all grade levels was five. The third most frequently used team size was three at the fifth and sixth grade levels and six or more at the seventh and eighth grade levels. Two-teacher teams were found in about 15% of middle schools at the fifth and sixth grade level and 4% at the seventh and eighth grade levels.

FIGURE 1
PERCENT OF MIDDLE SCHOOLS USING TEAM ORGANIZATION
1988, 1993, 2001

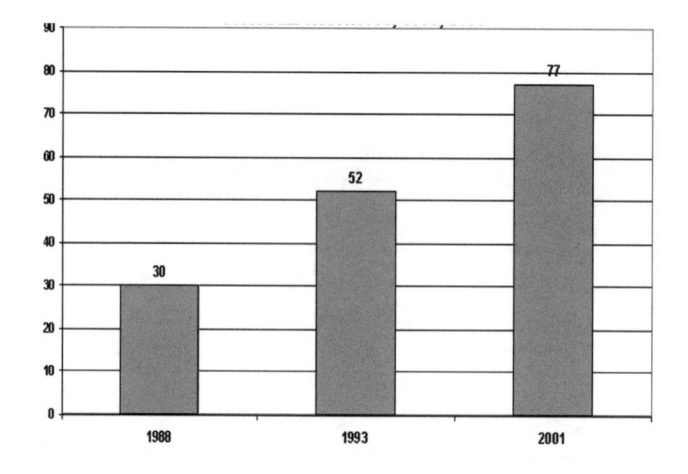

TABLE 9
PERCENT OF SCHOOLS UTILIZING SELECTED TEAM SIZES
BY GRADE LEVEL

Team Size	Fifth	Sixth	Seventh	Eighth
Two	16	15	4	4
Three	22	20	11	10
Four	35	28	39	37
Five	27	22	30	31
Six or more	0	15	16	18
Total	100	100	100	100

In summary, fifth and sixth grade teams are more likely to consist of three, four, and five-teacher teams (84% and 70% respectively) with grades seven and eight more frequently consisting of four, five, and six-teacher teams (85% and 86% respectively). Approximately 15% of middle schools reported that sixth, seventh, and eighth grade teams were made up of six or more teachers, and about 15% utilized two-teacher teams at the fifth and sixth grade levels. Respondents from 69% of schools indicated that teachers of exceptional students served as team members at their schools.

The number of planning periods provided each week for those teaching on teams was examined. The most common plans were five (40%) or ten (41%) periods per week (Table 10). The remaining 19% of schools used a variety of plans with 5% reporting teachers had no common planning time.

TABLE 10
PERCENT OF COMMON PLANNING PERIODS PER WEEK

Common Planning Periods	Percent
None	5
Ten	41
Nine	1
Eight	3
Seven	1
Six	1
Five	40
Four	0
Three	4
Two	1
One	3
Total	100

Having team leaders for interdisciplinary teams is common practice in middle schools. Only 11% of schools in the present study did not utilize team leaders, which represents a 9% decrease since 1993 (20%) (Table 11). The most common method of selecting team leaders was by appointment by the principal (33%). This represents a change from the 1993 study where the most common method of selecting team leaders was "election by the team" (26%). Election by the team was the second most frequently used method for selecting team leaders in 2001 (23%), and appointment by the principal was the second most common method in 1993. When the two most frequently used methods of selecting team leaders in the 2001 study are combined, 56% of all middle schools either had team leaders appointed by the principal or elected by team members. Fifteen percent (15%) of respondents reported that team leadership is rotated among team members, and 14% indicated that team leaders emerge informally.

TABLE 11
PERCENT OF SELECTION METHODS FOR TEAM LEADERS:
1993 AND 2001

Selection Methods	1993	2001
Appointed by principal	24	33
Elected by team	26	23
Rotate among team members	16	15
Emerge informally	11	14
No team leaders	20	11
Other	3	4
Total	100	100

Remedial Instruction Arrangements

The 1993 and 2001 surveys collected information about the ways middle schools provide remediation opportunities for students (Figure 2). These features ranged from "extra work being assigned" to more formal organizational approaches such as "tutoring before and after school" and "Saturday classes." Although increases were found in all remedial arrangements listed, the most significant increases were found in the categories of "summer school" (22%), "extra period" (21%), and "tutoring before or after school" (20%). The data made it evident that middle schools typically offer several remedial opportunities. Comparative data were not available for "tutoring during the school day" since it was a new item added to the study. However, 47% of middle schools reported using this remediation plan.

FIGURE 2
PERCENT OF SPECIAL REMEDIAL ARRANGEMENTS
1993 AND 2001

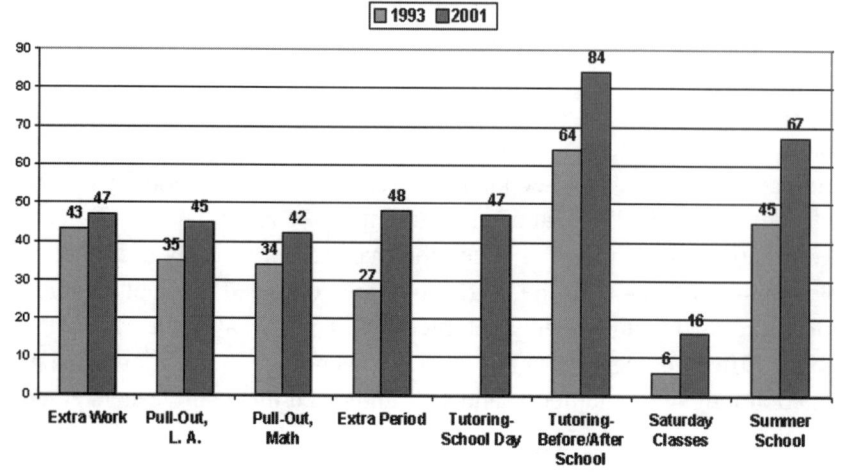

Category	1993	2001
Extra Work	43	47
Pull-Out, L.A.	35	45
Pull-Out, Math	34	42
Extra Period	27	48
Tutoring-School Day	—	47
Tutoring-Before/After School	64	84
Saturday Classes	6	16
Summer School	45	67

Scheduling Plans

The current study examined scheduling plans for middle schools and compared the results with those from the 1993 study (Table 12). Selected comparisons were also made with the 1968 study. It should be noted that respondents were asked to indicate all scheduling options that applied to their schools (e.g., uniform periods and self-contained) meaning that totals for columns do not add to 100%. This also makes comparisons with past studies difficult since multiple responses make percentages in respective columns higher than if selecting a single option. However, data collected make it possible to determine the predominate methods of scheduling in today's middle schools.

TABLE 12
PERCENT OF SCHEDULING PLANS UTILIZED BY SCHOOLS: 1993 AND 2001

Scheduling Plan	Fifth		Sixth		Seventh		Eighth	
	1993	2001	1993	2001	1993	2001	1993	2001
Self Contained	30	18	13	10	9	9	7	9
Uniform Periods	49	55	82	56	86	75	89	76
Flexible Block	32	17	39	21	34	23	25	23
Daily-Varying	8	17	7	11	5	11	4	11

The use of uniform periods remains the most popular way to organize middle schools. However, with the exception of fifth grade, the use of uniform periods has decreased in the eight-year period (26% in sixth grade, 11% in seventh grade, 13% in eighth grade) since the 1993 study. This trend reverses the one found between the 1988 and 1993 studies where the use of uniform daily periods had increased by about 4%. Seventeen percent (17%) of middle schools reported the use of flexible block schedules in fifth grade, 21% in sixth grade, and 23% in grades seven and eight. Respondents were also asked to indicate how many periods were used at their schools for each grade level. Ninety percent (90%) of schools used seven or eight period days for the fifth grade, 79% for sixth grade, and 80% for grades seven and eight (Table 13). Sixth period days were the next most popular plan with very few schools using five-period days at any grade level (about 3%).

TABLE 13
PERCENT OF SCHOOLS UTILIZING SELECTED NUMBER OF
DAILY UNIFORM PERIODS

Grade	Five Periods	Six Periods	Seven Periods	Eight Periods
Fifth	4	6	37	53
Sixth	3	18	35	44
Seventh	2	17	39	41
Eighth	3	17	39	41

Seventeen percent (17%) of schools reported using daily periods of varying lengths in fifth grade and 11% at the sixth, seventh, and eighth grade levels. This represents an increase since the 1993 study, which found that approximately 5% of schools used this scheduling plan. With the exception of fifth grade (30% to 18%), the percentage of schools using self-contained classrooms did not change significantly as compared with results from the 1993 study.

In summary, with 77% of middle schools indicating that interdisciplinary team organization is utilized in their school (Figure 1), it is clear that these schools are utilizing a variety of scheduling plans that make this instructional plan possible. With about one-third of these schools reporting that either a flexible block schedule or periods of varying lengths are used, it seems logical to assume that that many of the schools reporting the use of uniform periods are blocking several of these periods together to accommodate interdisciplinary team organization.

Time Allotted for Core Instruction

Respondents were asked to provide information regarding the number of minutes per week and weeks per year devoted to instruction in each of the core subjects at their schools (science, language arts, social studies, mathematics). To simplify comparisons, the mean number of minutes each subject is taught at each grade level was calculated. This method took into account that various kinds of scheduling were being utilized (e.g., 45-minute periods all year, 90-minute blocks for one-half year). This item was new to this survey, and therefore no comparative data from past studies are available.

Language arts received the largest number of minutes for instruction at all grade levels, with mathematics being allocated the second largest number of minutes (Figure 3). Science and social studies had fewer minutes than the other two core subject areas, but the times provided were not dramatically different from those provided for mathematics instruction. At the fifth grade level, the average (mean) number of minutes allocated daily for language arts instruction was 72. This allocation of time dropped to 67 minutes for grade six, 62 minutes for grade seven, and 61 minutes for grade eight.

The data clearly demonstrate that the nation's middle schools allocate a large portion of instructional time to the traditional core (basic) subjects of language arts, science, social studies, and mathematics. The mean number of minutes allocated for instruction in core subjects in this study was three hours and 42 minutes at the fifth and sixth grade levels and three hours and thirty-five

Status and Progress 19

minutes at the seventh and eighth grade levels. Findings from this study also revealed that subjects not typically included in high stakes testing programs (e.g., social studies) were not receiving significantly less instructional time as compared to the tested ones (e.g., mathematics).

FIGURE 3
MEAN INSTRUCTIONAL MINUTES PER DAY
IN CORE SUBJECTS

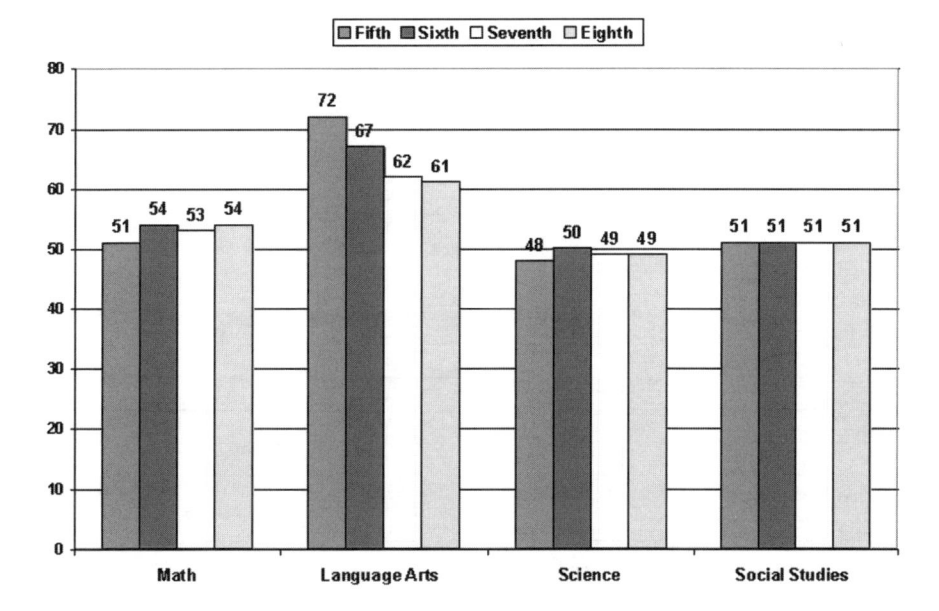

Subject	Fifth	Sixth	Seventh	Eighth
Math	51	54	53	54
Language Arts	72	67	62	61
Science	48	50	49	49
Social Studies	51	51	51	51

Other Required Subjects

Table 14 provides a comprehensive listing of required and elective subjects provided by middle schools participating in this study. Table 15 includes data from the 1993 study so that comparisons can be made. The core areas of language arts, science, social studies, and mathematics are not included in the tables since these core subjects were required at all middle schools. The seventh grade has been selected as the focus of discussion here. Readers are encouraged to examine data in Tables 14 and 15 for information about other grade levels.

TABLE 14
PERCENT OF SCHOOLS OFFERING REQUIRED AND
ELECTIVE SUBJECTS: 2001

Subjects	Required 5th	Required 6th	Required 7th	Required 8th	Elective 5th	Elective 6th	Elective 7th	Elective 8th
Agriculture	0	0	1	1	0	0	4	6
Art	75	39	47	41	16	86	54	47
Band	0	0	0	0	62	82	85	85
Career Education	17	14	15	21	5	12	13	16
Chorus	0	0	0	0	34	58	70	72
Computers	65	52	48	40	9	27	35	41
Creative Writing	27	12	12	12	3	5	6	7
Fam./Con. Science	12	26	29	25	2	14	20	25
Foreign Language	20	23	23	24	6	19	35	46
General Music	71	41	29	24	15	22	18	17
Health	54	58	62	58	8	11	13	13
Industrial Arts	19	25	32	27	3	12	23	29
Journalism	0	0	1	2	3	4	12	20
Life Skills	15	17	15	14	2	10	14	15
Orchestra	0	0	0	0	12	26	72	72
Physical Education	94	91	88	83	6	9	12	17
Reading	81	68	53	46	8	13	15	16
Sex Education	17	24	25	27	4	5	5	6
Speech	7	4	5	5	8	4	8	10
Word Processing	30	20	16	14	2	10	12	14
Other	11	10	10	10	4	1	13	15

TABLE 15
PERCENT OF SCHOOLS OFFERING REQUIRED AND
ELECTIVE SUBJECTS: 1993

Subjects	Required				Elective			
	5th	6th	7th	8th	5th	6th	7th	8th
Agriculture	1	1	1	1	1	1	3	5
Art	74	61	45	33	14	28	53	54
Band	0	0	0	0	58	90	93	93
Career Education	1	8	12	15	3	8	11	15
Chorus	0	0	0	0	14	59	75	79
Computers	46	42	40	34	10	28	29	39
Creative Writing	24	27	25	24	3	4	8	10
Fam./Con. Science	21	32	36	28	5	15	35	47
Foreign Language	15	14	14	14	6	15	39	50
General Music	67	48	32	21	6	21	22	21
Health	67	66	66	64	1	4	6	7
Industrial Arts	18	31	34	29	3	17	35	47
Journalism	0	0	0	0	3	6	17	27
Orchestra	0	0	0	0	17	33	38	38
Reading	87	82	61	52	2	3	12	14
Sex Education	44	43	41	42	4	4	5	6
Speech	0	0	0	0	3	6	13	15
Word Processing	7	8	8	10	7	5	11	15

In addition to the core subjects, several other subjects are frequently required in the nation's middle schools (Figure 4). In the 2001 study, the most frequently required subject at the seventh grade level was physical education (88%), followed by health (62%), and reading (53%). Computers and art were also leading choices for required subjects (48% and 47% respectively). Other seventh grade subjects required in one-fourth or more of schools in the study included industrial education (32%), general music (29%), family and consumer sciences (29%), and sex education (25%).

Data collected regarding physical education were different in the 1988 and 1993 surveys than in the present study. Respondents in the previous studies were asked to indicate whether or not all students took physical education all year. Therefore, comparative data were not available regarding the frequency of offering physical education as a required subject. It is clear, however, that physical education continues to be required in the large majority of middle schools at all grade levels. At the seventh grade level, 88% of middle schools required physical education with the remaining 12% offering it as an elective subject. Even higher percentages of middle schools required physical education at the fifth (94%) and sixth (91%) grade levels.

FIGURE 4
PERCENT OF MOST FREQUENTLY REQUIRED NON-CORE SEVENTH GRADE COURSES

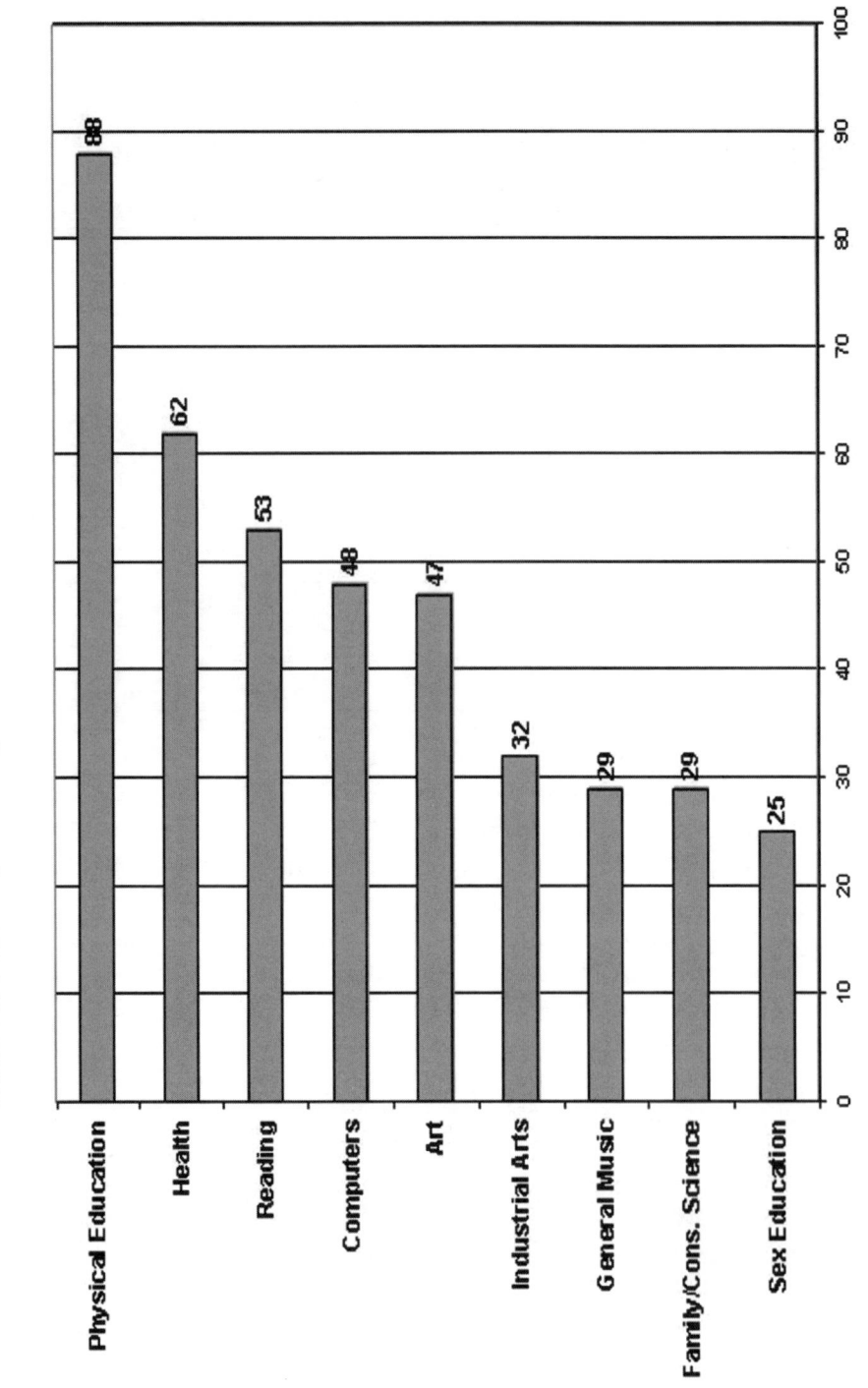

Course	Percent
Physical Education	88
Health	62
Reading	53
Computers	48
Art	47
Industrial Arts	32
General Music	29
Family/Cons. Science	29
Sex Education	25

Subjects required in middle schools showed little change since the 1993 study with the eight most frequently required subjects being the same at the seventh grade level (Tables 14 and 15). There were some increases and decreases in the percentage of schools requiring these subjects. Eight percent (8%) more schools required computers (48%), and 2% more required art (47%). The largest decrease found in these most frequently required subjects was in sex education with a 16% decrease (41% to 25% respectively). Additionally, 8% fewer schools offered reading as a required subject at the seventh grade level. Family and consumer science, health, industrial arts, and music were also required in smaller percentages of schools.

Elective Subjects Offered

The range of elective courses offered in middle schools had changed little since the 1993 study. Once again using seventh grade for discussion purposes, band (85%), orchestra (72%), chorus (70%), and art (54%) were the most frequently offered electives. These were followed in popularity by computers (35%), foreign language (35%), industrial arts (23%), and family and consumer science (20%) (Figure 5). Readers are encouraged to see Tables 14 and 15 for information about other elective subjects and grade levels.

The largest change in the percentage of schools offering elective courses was found in orchestra, which had increased from 38% to 70%. The only other increases were found in computers (6%) and art (1%). Decreases at the seventh grade level were the greatest in the subjects of family and consumer science (15%), industrial arts (12%), and band (8%).

Interest Class/Mini-Course Programs

Data were also collected on interest class/mini-course programs. The survey instrument defined interest classes/mini-course programs as "a short-term, student interest-centered course." Forty-nine percent (49%) of schools reported having these programs. This represents an 18% increase since the 1993 study (31%) (Table 16). Information regarding the frequency of scheduling interest/mini-class programs was also collected. The number of weeks interest class/mini-course programs were offered ranged from 1 to 44 with the average being 15 weeks. Programs were offered from one to five times per week with the mean number of days being four. The average number of days per year these programs were offered was 64.

FIGURE 5
PERCENT OF MOST FREQUENTLY OFFERED SEVENTH GRADE ELECTIVE COURSES

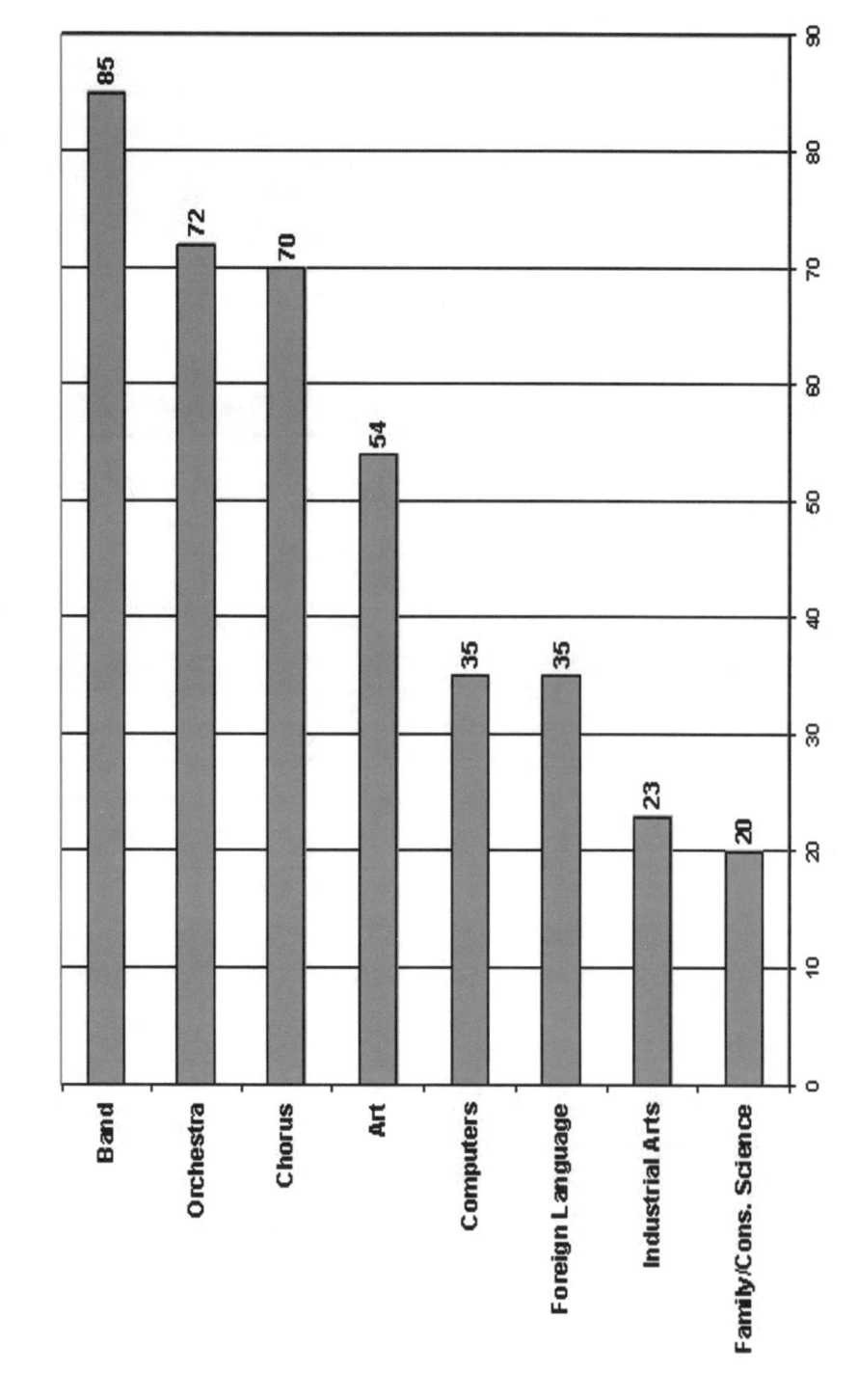

Course	Percent
Band	85
Orchestra	72
Chorus	70
Art	54
Computers	35
Foreign Language	35
Industrial Arts	23
Family/Cons. Science	20

TABLE 16
PERCENT OF SCHOOLS WITH MINI-COURSE PROGRAMS:
1993 AND 2001

Mini-Courses	1993	2001
Yes	31	49
No	69	51
Total	100	100

The survey instrument also listed selected themes for these programs and provided the opportunity for additional themes to be added. As shown in Table 17, the most popular themes for interest class/mini-course programs were technology (93%) and fine arts (90%). The majority of schools also identified the themes of performing arts (70%), academics (66%), foreign language and culture (60%), and personal development (58%). Sports, crafts, and community service were also popular themes.

TABLE 17
PERCENT OF SCHOOLS UTILIZING SELECTED
MINI-COURSE THEMES

Themes	Percent
Technology	93
Fine arts	90
Performing arts	70
Academic	66
Foreign languages and culture	60
Personal development	58
Sports	48
Crafts	43
Community service	33

Teacher-Based Guidance (Advisory) Programs

Teacher-based guidance programs – known by a variety of names such as advisory programs, homebase, and homeroom – are widely recognized as essential components of developmentally responsive middle schools (National Middle School Association, 1995; Jenkins & Daniel, 2000). As shown in Figure 6, the percentage of middle schools with advisory programs increased 8% from 1988 to 1993 and an additional 1% by 2001. It is evident from the data that the majority of middle schools have failed to implement advisory programs.

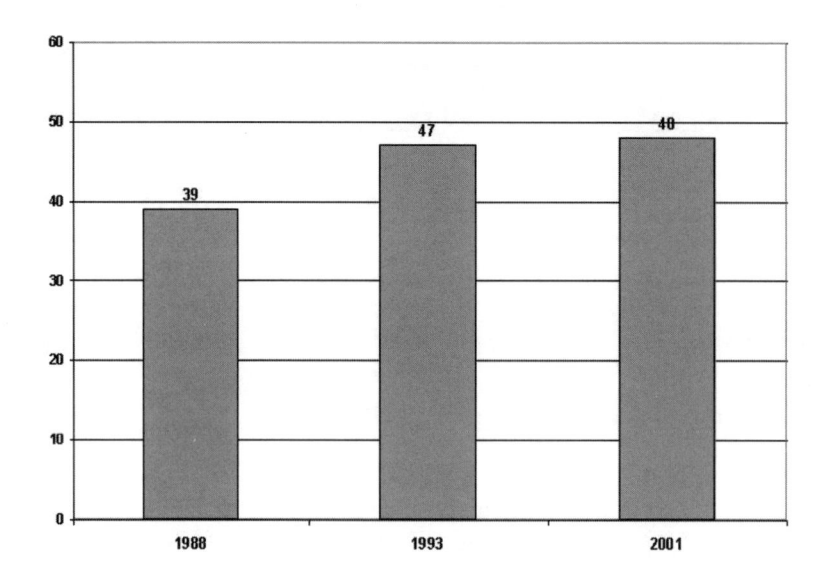

FIGURE 6
PERCENT OF SCHOOLS WITH ADVISORY PROGRAMS:
1988, 1993, AND 2001

Year	Percent
1988	39
1993	47
2001	48

Respondents provided additional information about advisory programs at their schools. Data revealed that in middle schools with advisory programs, the large majority of all teachers served as advisors (85%). The majority (54%) of schools scheduled advisory periods lasting from 16 to 30 minutes (Table 18). Nineteen percent (19%) of middle schools reported scheduling up to 15 minutes for advisory, 20% 31 to 45 minutes, and 7% more than 45 minutes. Middle schools scheduled advisories for longer meeting times than was the case in the 1988 study when 59% of schools scheduled 16 or more minutes. Middle schools scheduling meeting times for 15 minutes or less decreased significantly since the 1988 study (40% to 19%). However, little change in scheduling patterns occurred between 1988 and 2001.

TABLE 18
PERCENT OF MINUTES ADVISORY SCHEDULED: 1988, 1993, AND 2001

Number of Minutes	1988	1993	2001
1-15	40	15	19
16-30	42	65	54
31-45	10	15	20
More than 45	7	5	7

The number of days per week middle schools scheduled advisory periods was also examined. The percentage of middle schools having advisory groups meet daily decreased when compared to results from the 1988 and 1993 studies (Table 19). Seventy-eight percent (78%) of schools scheduled daily advisory meetings in 1988, 63% in 1993, and 56% in 2001. The majority of middle schools with advisory programs in the present study reported having daily advisory meetings (56%). There was also an increase in the percentage of schools that hold advisory sessions one or two times per week (approximately 20% in 1988 and 1993 and 32% in 2001).

TABLE 19
PERCENT OF FREQUENCY OF ADVISORY MEETINGS: 1988, 1993, AND 2001

Frequency	1988	1993	2001
Five Days Per Week	78	63	56
Four Days Per Week	1	2	<1
Three Days Per Week	3	4	2
Two Days Per Week	9	6	16
One Day Per Week	10	14	16
Twice Per Month	-	5	2
Other	-	6	8

Interschool Sports

The issue of the appropriateness of interschool sports at the middle school level has long been debated (Gerdy, 2000; McEwin & Dickinson, 1998). However, data from this study clearly document that competitive interschool sports are played at the vast majority of middle schools in the nation. Ninety-six percent (96%) of schools in the present study reported having interschool sports programs (Figure 7). This is a significant increase since the 1968 study. Fifty percent (50%) of schools reported having interschool sports programs then as compared to 77% in 1988 and 1993. Therefore, the percentages of middle schools with interschool sports programs has increased 46% since 1968 and 19% since 1993.

FIGURE 7
PERCENT OF SCHOOLS WITH INTERSCHOOL SPORTS PROGRAMS:
1968, 1988, 1993, AND 2001

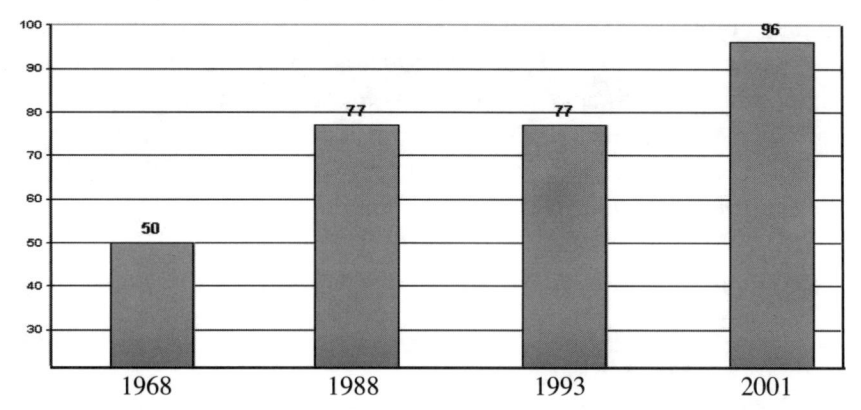

Year	Percent
1968	50
1988	77
1993	77
2001	96

Seventh grade is used as a focus in this discussion. The most frequently offered interschool sports for seventh grade boys were basketball (88%), track (71%), football (62%), wrestling and cross-country (45%), and soccer (33%) (Table 20; Figure 8). These were also the most frequently offered sports in 1988. The percentage of schools offering these sports increased somewhat since the 1993 study. Cross-country was found to be growing in popularity with 15% more schools offering this sport in 2001 than did so in 1993 (30% and 45% respectively).

TABLE 20
PERCENT OF SCHOOLS OFFERING SELECTED INTERSCHOOL SPORTS
PROGRAMS FOR BOYS: 1993 AND 2001

Sport	Fifth 1993	Fifth 2001	Sixth 1993	Sixth 2001	Seventh 1993	Seventh 2001	Eighth 1993	Eighth 2001
Baseball	3	<1	7	9	22	26	24	28
Basketball	13	12	24	29	82	88	86	90
Cross Country	4	10	13	19	30	45	32	45
Football	3	0	8	10	56	62	62	66
Gymnastics	0	0	2	1	3	2	3	2
Soccer	5	8	11	13	24	33	25	33
Softball	3	4	5	4	7	6	7	6
Swimming	4	1	4	4	9	10	9	10
Tennis	1	2	4	6	15	17	16	17
Track	8	7	23	27	70	71	72	73
Volleyball	2	3	7	8	11	14	12	14
Wrestling	6	4	11	16	41	45	43	47

FIGURE 8
PERCENT OF MOST FREQUENTLY OFFERED
SEVENTH GRADE GIRLS' AND BOYS' INTERSCHOOL SPORTS PROGRAMS

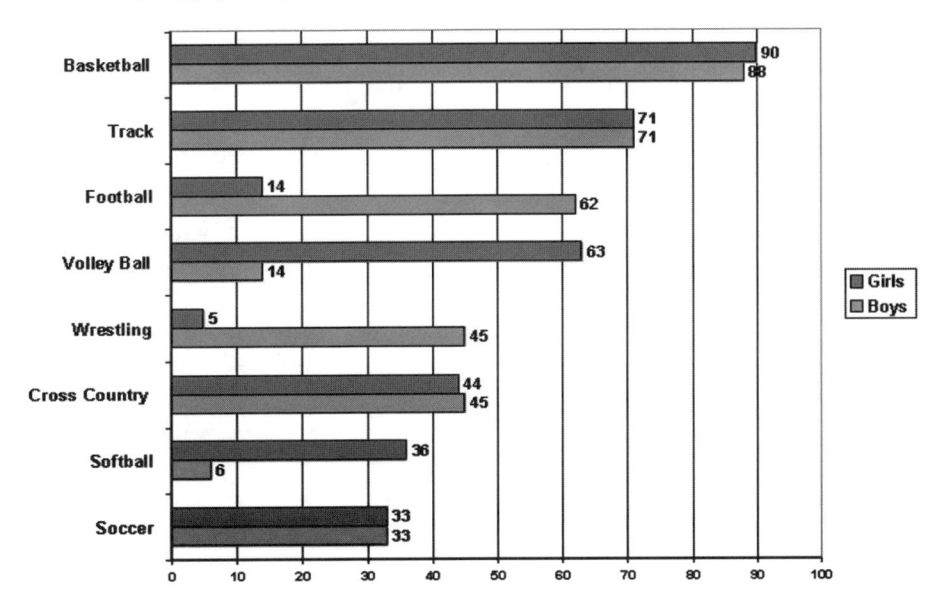

Sport	Girls	Boys
Basketball	90	88
Track	71	71
Football	14	62
Volley Ball	63	14
Wrestling	5	45
Cross Country	44	45
Softball	36	6
Soccer	33	33

Basketball was also the most frequently offered seventh grade interschool sport for girls (90%), followed by track (71%), volleyball (63%), cross-county (44%), and softball (36%) (Table 21; Figure 8). These were also the most frequently offered interschool sports for girls in the 1993 study. Soccer, although not one of the most frequently offered sports, had increased by 10% since 1993. Football and wrestling, traditionally considered by many as sports for boys, had been opened to girls in larger percentages of middle schools in 2001 than in 1993.

Respondents from 38% of middle schools in the study indicated that new interschool sports had been added at their schools. The most frequently added new interschool sports were soccer (29%), softball (17%), volleyball (16%), cross-country (15%), wrestling (13%), and track (12%) (Table 22). Smaller percentages of middle schools had added basketball, baseball, and golf.

TABLE 21
PERCENT OF SCHOOLS OFFERING SELECTED INTERSCHOOL SPORTS
PROGRAMS FOR GIRLS: 1993 AND 2001

Sport	Fifth 1993	Fifth 2001	Sixth 1993	Sixth 2001	Seventh 1993	Seventh 2001	Eighth 1993	Eighth 2001
Baseball	1	1	1	2	3	4	3	7
Basketball	12	12	24	29	81	90	84	90
Cross Country	4	9	13	19	30	44	32	46
Football	1	0	1	4	6	14	7	15
Gymnastics	2	1	3	2	7	5	17	5
Soccer	5	7	10	13	22	33	23	33
Softball	6	6	11	12	29	36	32	38
Swimming	4	1	4	4	9	10	10	10
Tennis	1	2	4	6	15	17	16	17
Track	8	7	23	27	70	71	72	73
Volleyball	5	3	15	18	57	63	59	73
Wrestling	1	3	2	8	2	16	5	17

TABLE 22
NUMBER AND PERCENT OF CHANGES IN INTERSCHOOL
SPORTS PROGRMS

Changes	Number	Percent
No Changes	328	46
Eliminated Some Sports	46	6
Added New Sports	270	38
Reduced Number of Games	27	4
Play Only Schools in District	53	7
Play Adjacent District Schools	46	6

Interdisciplinary Instruction

Table 23 provides data from the 1993 and 2001 studies on estimates of the percentages of interdisciplinary instruction used in middle level schools. The largest percentage of schools (44%) reported using interdisciplinary instruction from 1% to 20% of the instructional day. Additionally, the number of schools represented in the 21-40% category increased by 11% (24% and 35% respectively). There was little change in the percentages of schools selecting the responses of 61% and higher. Overall, the results indicate that larger percentages of middle schools used interdisciplinary instruction more frequently than was the case in the earlier studies.

Status and Progress

TABLE 23
PERCENT OF INTERDISCIPLINARY INSTRUCTION: 1993 AND 2001

Percent of Interdisciplinary Instruction	1993	2001
1-20	60	44
21-40	24	35
41-60	8	12
61-80	5	6
81-100	3	3
Total	100	100

Use of Selected Instructional Strategies

Respondents from the 1993 and 2001 studies provided information on the use of selected instructional strategies at their schools (Table 24). Specifically, they were asked how often their schools used:
- Direct instruction (teacher presentation, drill, practice, etc.)
- Cooperative learning (structured group work and rewards for achievement)
- Inquiry teaching (gathering information, deriving conclusions)
- Independent study (working individually on selected or assigned tasks).

The options provided on the survey included the responses of "rarely or never," "occasionally," and "regularly."

The most frequently used instructional strategy at all grade levels was direct instruction. Eighty-five percent (85%) of schools reported its use on a regular basis at the fifth grade level, 87% at the sixth grade level, and 88% at the seventh and eighth grade levels. These percentages are comparable to those reported in the 1993 study (Table 24).

Comparison of data from the two studies revealed an increase in the use of cooperative learning on a regular basis at all grade levels (Figure 9). This increase averaged 10% with the largest increases occurring at the fifth (12%) and eighth (11%) grade levels.

Increases were also found in the percentages of schools using independent study as an instructional strategy on a regular basis. The largest gain was 25% in grade five, followed by 13% in grade six, and 12% in grades seven and eight. Additionally the use of inquiry teaching increased at all grade levels. The percentages of schools reporting using this instructional strategy on a regular basis increased 8% at the fifth and sixth grade levels, 10% at the seventh grade level, and 11% at the eighth grade level.

TABLE 24
PERCENT OF SCHOOLS UTILIZING SELECTED TYPES OF
INSTRUCTIONAL STRATEGIES: 1993 AND 2001

Fifth

Type of Instruction	1993 RA	1993 OC	1993 RG	2001 RA	2001 OC	2001 RG
Direct Instruction	2	12	86	2	13	85
Cooperative Learning	3	46	51	3	34	63
Inquiry Teaching	13	59	28	6	58	36
Independent Study	39	48	13	19	43	38

Sixth

Type of Instruction	1993 RA	1993 OC	1993 RG	2001 RA	2001 OC	2001 RG
Direct Instruction	1	10	88	1	12	87
Cooperative Learning	3	43	54	1	38	61
Inquiry Teaching	9	56	34	8	50	42
Independent Study	31	51	18	18	51	31

Seventh

Type of Instruction	1993 RA	1993 OC	1993 RG	2001 RA	2001 OC	2001 RG
Direct Instruction	1	9	90	1	11	88
Cooperative Learning	3	47	50	<1	40	60
Inquiry Teaching	10	56	35	0	48	45
Independent Study	29	51	20	17	51	32

Eighth

Type of Instruction	1993 RA	1993 OC	1993 RG	2001 RA	2001 OC	2001 RG
Direct Instruction	1	8	91	1	11	88
Cooperative Learning	4	48	48	1	40	59
Inquiry Teaching	10	56	34	8	47	45
Independent Study	29	51	20	17	51	32

RA: Rarely or Never   OC: Occasionally   RG: Regularly

FIGURE 9
PERCENT OF SCHOOLS UTILIZING COOPERATIVE LEARNING ON A REGULAR BASIS:
1993 AND 2001

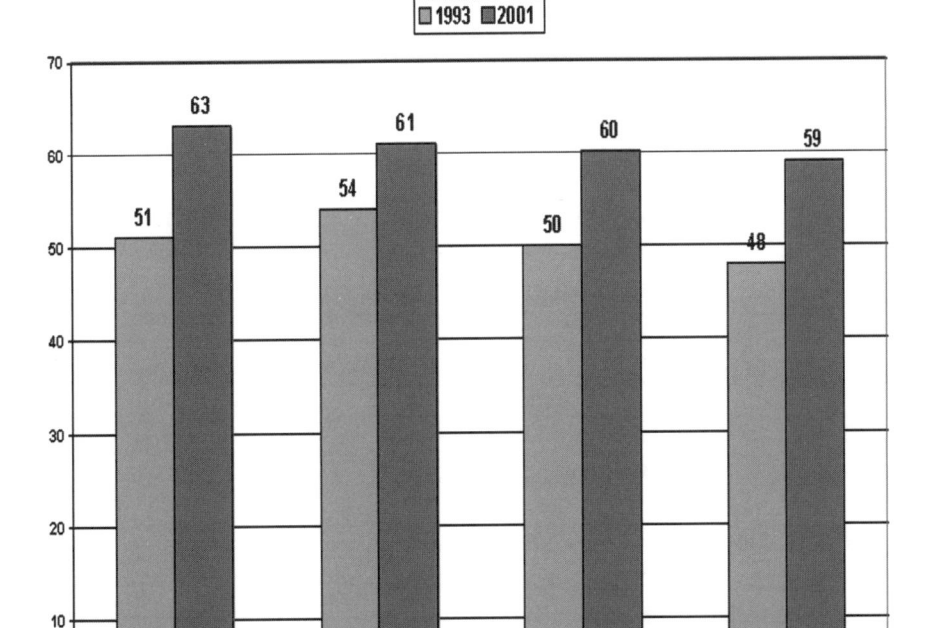

Grade	1993	2001
Fifth	51	63
Sixth	54	61
Seventh	50	60
Eighth	48	59

Inquiry teaching was the most frequently selected choice for occasional use of an instructional strategy. Responses in this category showed a 1% to 9% decrease from those found in the 1993 study. Fifty-eight percent (58%) of schools reported occasional use of inquiry teaching at the fifth grade level, 50% at the sixth grade level, 48% at the seventh grade level, and 47% at the eighth grade level. The occasional use of independent study as an instructional strategy decreased by 5% at the fifth grade level, but remained the same at the other grade levels (51%). The occasional use of direct instruction decreased about 2% from the 1993 study with the occasional use of cooperative learning decreasing about 8%. It should be noted, however, that these decreases were paralleled by increases in the use of these instructional strategies on a regular basis.

The instructional strategy most frequently selected as rarely or never used was independent study. However, the percentages of schools had decreased since the 1993 study at all grade levels (20% in grade five and about 12% in grades seven and eight). This indicates larger percentages of middle schools are utilizing independent study as an instructional strategy. Percentages of schools reporting the occasional use of inquiry teaching followed a similar pattern (Table 24). Only small changes were found in the percentages of schools utilizing direct instruction and cooperative learning on an occasional or never basis.

Instructional Grouping Practices

Seventy-eight percent (78%) of respondents reported tracking was used in one or more core subjects at their schools (Table 25). This represents a 10% increase in the percentage of middle schools tracking students in core subjects since the 1993 study (68% and 78% respectively). The most frequently tracked subject was mathematics (Table 26). Seventy-three percent (73%) of middle schools track in mathematics with the second most frequently tracked subject being language arts (28%). Twenty-three percent (23%) of middle schools reported using tracking in reading. Only 12% of schools tracked in science and 10% in social studies.

TABLE 25
PERCENT OF ABILITY GROUPING/TRACKING PRACTICES: 1993 AND 2001

Ability Grouping/Tracking Plan	1993	2001
None	32	22
All grades - all basic subjects	4	6
All grades – certain subjects	37	35
Certain grades – all subjects	2	<1
Certain grades – certain subjects	24	24

TABLE 26
PERCENT OF SCHOOLS ABILITY GROUPING/TRACKING IN
SELECTED SUBJECTS

Subject	Percent
Mathematics	73
Language Arts	28
Reading	23
Science	12
Social Studies	10

Information was also collected regarding operating policies in schools that tracked students (Table 25). Categories used in this survey item included the following:
- Ability grouping (tracking) used at all grade levels in all basic subjects
- Ability grouping (tracking) used at all grade levels, but restricted to certain subjects
- Ability grouping (tracking) is used only at certain grade levels, but in all subject areas
- Ability grouping (tracking) is used at certain grade levels, but restricted to certain subjects
- Other.

Respondents were asked to select the one statement that best described the operating policy at their school. The most frequently used operating policy for tracking in middle schools was "all grades, certain subjects. Thirty-five percent (35%) of middle schools followed this policy as compared to 37% in the 1993 study. Twenty-four percent (24%) of middle schools used the policy of "certain grades, certain subjects," a percentage identical to that found in the 1993 study. Only 6% of middle schools tracked in "all grades, all subjects" which represents a 2% increase since 1993.

Student Progress Reports

Middle schools reported using a great variety of mechanisms for reporting student progress. The most frequently used method of reporting student progress continued to be use of a letter scale. Over 80% of middle schools in the 1968, 1988, 1993, and 2001 studies indicated use of the method (Table 27). Holding parent conferences was also a popular method of reporting student progress with 69% of middle schools utilizing this plan. This percentage has remained rather consistent since the 1988 study.

The use of informal notes also continues to be popular with 62% of schools using this method. The use of percentage marks has increased since earlier studies (46%). Word scales were used by 20% of middle schools and number scales by 9%. Portfolios were utilized in 30% of schools, which was an 8% increase since the 1993 study.

TABLE 27
PERCENT OF SCHOOLS UTILIZING SELECTED METHODS OF REPORTING
PUPIL PROGRESS: 1968, 1988, 1993, AND 2001

Method	1968	1988	1993	2001
Letter scale	86	85	80	84
Word scale	6	21	20	20
Number scale	13	13	10	9
Percentage marks	36	29	32	46
S/U	26	39	38	41
Informal notes	46	64	60	62
Parent conferences	42	67	62	69
Portfolio	-	-	22	30

Faculty

Data from the present study show that some progress has been made in employing middle level teachers who have had specialized middle level professional preparation (Table 28 and Figure 10). Respondents were asked to select one of the following categories that best described the percentage of teachers at their schools who had received specialized middle level teacher preparation:
- Less than 25%
- 25-50%
- 51-75%
- 76-100%.

TABLE 28
PERCENT OF TEACHERS WITH SPECIALIZED MIDDLE
LEVEL TEACHER PREPARATION: 1988, 1993, AND 2001

Percent With Special Preparation	Percent of Schools		
	1988	1993	2001
Less than 25	58	62	45
25-50	17	18	17
51-75	13	11	15
76-100	13	9	24

Respondents at 24% of middle schools indicated that from 76% to 100% of teachers had received specialized middle level teacher preparation. This represents an increase of 15% since the 1993 study. There was also 4% increase in the 51% to 75% category. The percentage of middle schools having 25% to 50% had remained constant since 1988. The percentage of schools having less that 25% with specialized professional preparation had decreased as the percentage with specialized professional preparation increased. Respondents from 45% of schools indicated this category as compared with 58% in 1998 and 62% in 1993.

FIGURE 10
PERCENT OF TEACHERS WITH SPECIALIZED MIDDLE LEVEL TEACHER PREPARATION:
1988, 1993, AND 2001

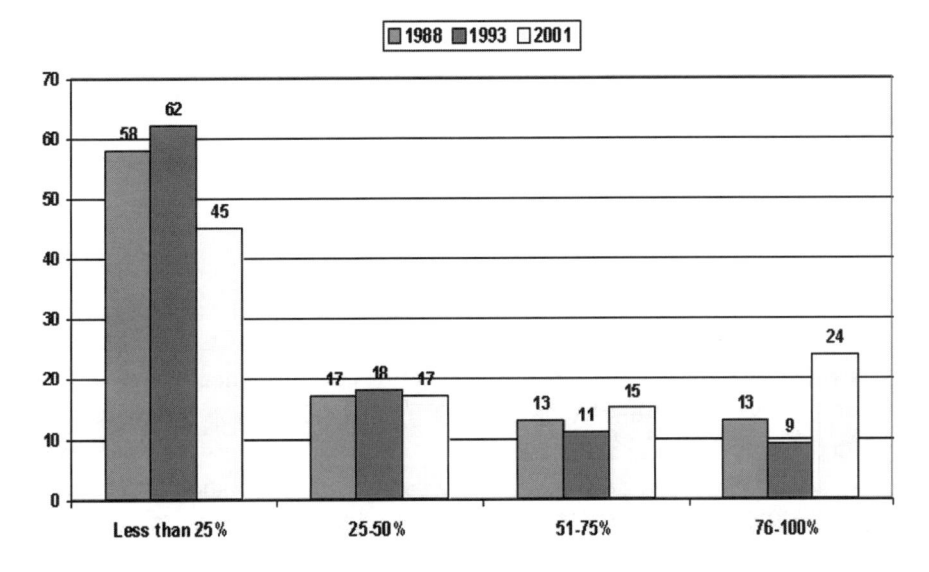

	1988	1993	2001
Less than 25%	58	62	45
25-50%	17	18	17
51-75%	13	11	15
76-100%	13	9	24

When asked to estimate the percentage of teachers wishing to leave the middle level, 51% of respondents in the present study believed that no teachers at their schools wished to leave the middle level (Table 29). This represents an 11% increase since the 1993 study. Forty-six percent (46%) believed that 1% to 20% of teachers wished to leave the middle level leaving only 3% indicating that 21 or more percent wished to leave.

TABLE 29
PERCENT OF TEACHERS WISHING TO LEAVE THE MIDDLE LEVEL
1993 AND 2001

Percent Wishing to Leave	1993	2001
None	40	51
1-20	54	46
21-40	4	2
41-60	1	1
61-80	1	0
81-100	1	0
Total	101	100

High Stakes Testing

Two survey items focusing on the perceptions of respondents of the effects of the widespread implementation of high stakes testing programs were included for the first time in the 2001 survey. Table 30 presents the percentages of respondents' views regarding the impact of high stakes testing programs on selected middle school components. The majority of respondents believed that high stakes testing had influenced middle school components in positive or negative ways. The only component where the majority (58%) of respondents believed that high stakes testing had no impact was advisory programs. Twenty-seven percent (27%) perceived that high stakes testing had resulted in a positive impact on advisory programs and 15% a negative impact. Over one-third perceived that high stakes testing had no effect on electives, scheduling, teaming, and teacher planning time.

Eighty-one percent (81%) of respondents indicated that they thought high stakes testing has had a positive impact on curriculum and remediation at their schools. Seventy-four percent (74%) also perceived a positive impact on student learning and instructional delivery. Additionally, 53% of respondents believed high stakes testing had positively impacted instructional grouping practices. One-third or more also perceived high stakes testing has had a positive impact on teaming (48%), school climate (45%), scheduling (42%), and electives (33%).

Status and Progress 39

TABLE 30
PERCENT OF SCHOOLS REPORTING VARYING LEVELS OF IMPACT OF
HIGH STAKES TESTING ON SELECTED MIDDLE SCHOOL COMPONENTS

Components	No Impact	Positive Impact	Negative Impact
Advisory programs	58	27	15
Curriculum	6	81	14
Electives	36	33	31
Instructional delivery	8	74	17
Instructional grouping	30	53	17
Remediation	11	81	8
Scheduling	36	42	22
School climate	15	45	41
Student learning	10	74	16
Teacher planning time	34	41	25
Teaming	36	48	17

Forty-one percent (41%) of respondents believed that high stakes testing had a negative impact on school climate and 31% on electives. The next highest percentages were in the categories of teacher planning time (25%) and scheduling (22%). Seventeen percent (17%) also believed high stakes testing had a negative impact on instructional delivery, instructional grouping, and teaming. Responses in the remaining categories ranged from 8% to 16%. Overall, with all components considered, about 25% of respondents believed that high stakes had no impact on middle school components, 55% a positive impact, and 20% a negative impact.

Respondents were also asked to indicate the effects of high stakes testing on the use of time at their schools. Five categories were listed with choices for each being "no change," "increased time," or "decreased time" (Table 31). Sixty percent (60%) or more indicated no change for advisory programs (72%), electives (61%), and teacher planning (60%). Thirty percent (30%) of respondents indicated no change for instruction and 20% for remediation.

TABLE 31
PERCENT OF SCHOOLS REPORTING VARYING LEVELS OF HIGH STAKES
TESTING ON THE USE OF TIME

Components	No Change	Increased Time	Decreased Time
Advisory programs	72	11	18
Electives	61	6	33
Instruction	30	58	12
Remediation	20	75	5
Teacher planning	60	23	17

The largest percentages of respondents indicated that high stakes testing had resulted in increased time for remediation (75%) and instruction (58%). Twenty-three percent (23%) of schools had also increased teacher planning time. Only 11% reported increased time for advisory and 6% for electives. One-third of respondents indicated that electives received less instructional time as a result of high stakes testing, followed by advisory programs (18%), teacher planning (17%), instruction (12%), and remediation (5%).

Overall results reveal that respondents indicated that high stakes testing has resulted in more time being provided for remediation (75%) and instruction (58%), with much smaller percentages reporting decreased time (5% and 12% respectively). Eighteen percent (18%) indicated decreased time for advisory programs and 11% increased time. Electives seem to have lost the most significant amount of instructional time with 33% of schools reporting time for these subjects being decreased as the result of high stakes testing. Results in the category of teacher planning revealed that 23% reported increased time and 17% decreased time.◆

PART III

Conclusions and Recommendations

Grade Organization Trends, 44

School Size, 46

Team Organization, 48

Remedial Instruction Arrangements, 49

Scheduling Plans, 50

Time Allocated for Core Instruction, 51

Required Non-Core Subjects, 52

Elective Subjects, 52

Interest Class/Mini-Course Programs, 53

Teacher-Based Guidance (Advisory) Programs, 54

Interschool Sports Programs, 55

Interdisciplinary Instruction and Instructional Strategies, 56

Instructional Grouping Practices, 57

Student Progress Reports, 59

Faculty, 59

High Stakes Testing, 60

Concluding Statements, 64

Part III

Conclusions and Recommendations

This section presents conclusions drawn by the researchers using data from this study, other studies, and the middle school knowledge base. Recommendations are made following brief discussions of programs and practices addressed. Topics addressed in this section seem especially important to the future success of America's middle schools, and more importantly, to the young adolescents who depend on these schools to provide them with the knowledge, skills, and dispositions needed to become lifelong learners and productive citizens. Readers are encouraged to further explore the data in areas that reflect their special interests.

The term "middle school" is used throughout this section. However, this does not mean that the discussions and recommendations do not have significance for schools with other names or grade organizations (e.g., grades 7-9, K-8). Results from this study clearly have implications for middle level education in all schools that are responsible for the education and welfare of young adolescents.

The researchers have made no attempt to couch the conclusions and recommendations in either a positive or negative manner. The discussion is based on the premise that the weaknesses of middle school education should be acknowledged and remedied, and that accomplishments should be recognized and celebrated. How else can significant progress be made in the continuing struggle to provide all young adolescents with learning opportunities that are both academically rigorous and developmentally responsive?

The discussion and recommendations included in the chapter are also based on the belief that before significant, long-term reform of middle school education can become a reality, we must know the current status of the programs and practices that are prerequisite to providing high quality teaching and student learning. The researchers are well aware that simply having selected programs and practices at a middle school does not guarantee that the school is accomplishing its goal of providing all young adolescents with a high quality education. However, it is also understood that the existence of these programs and practices are crucial components of successful middle schools (e.g., interdisciplinary team organization and common teacher planning time).

Results from this study should provide guidance for those striving to establish highly effective middle schools as well as for those seeking to improve programs and practices in existing middle schools. The study also has implications for middle level programs in schools that include young adolescents in combination with other developmental age groups (e.g., grades K-8 or 7-12 schools).

For the purpose of organization, and to make it easier for readers to turn back to more detailed information if they wish, the following discussion is presented in the same order and uses virtually the same titles as the previous sections.

Grade Organization Trends

School districts throughout the nation have continued to move from a two-tier (e.g., K-8, 9-12) to a three-tier (e.g. K-5, 6-8, 9-12) organizational plan. There is widespread consensus that young adolescents enrolled in the middle grades need and deserve schools devoted exclusively to their education and welfare. With the exception of a minority of school districts, the overwhelming trend in school organization has been toward separately organized middle schools containing grades 5-8 and 6-8. As shown in Table 1, the number of grades 5-8 and 6-8 middle schools has steadily increased since the 1970s.

The most significant change in the grade organization of middle schools has been the dramatic decline of grades 7-9 junior high schools. For example, there were 4,711 public junior high schools in 1970 and only 632 by 2001 (Alexander & McEwin, 1989; Market Data Retrieval, 2001). This decline has resulted from many factors that are reflected in the literature and not discussed here (George & Alexander, 2003). However, it is certain that the overwhelming majority of educators and other stakeholders no longer view the junior high school as a viable choice for the education of young adolescents.

The number of grades 7-8 middle schools has also decreased in the last decade. This trend is, at least partially, the result of school districts having initially moved ninth grades to high schools with long-range plans to move sixth grades to middle schools whenever circumstances permitted. In many instances, this movement of sixth grade to the middle schools took several years since the plan often included new construction and/or major reorganizations of school districts.

The trend away from grades 7-8 middle schools is also likely due, in part, to the recognition of the importance of avoiding two-grade schools whenever possible. One problem with two-grade schools is that students attending those schools attend three different schools and make two transitions from one school to another in a period of less than four calendar years. It is important to recognize, however, that the barriers inherent in having two-grade middle schools can and have been overcome by many such schools across the nation.

Decreases in the number of grades 7-9, 7-8, and K-8 schools have been paralleled by increasing numbers of grades 5-8 and 6-8 middle schools (Alexander & McEwin, 1989; Market Data Retrieval, 2001). Data from a recent national survey of 1,423 middle and junior high school principals also reflect the support of educators for grades 6-8 middle schools. When these administrators were asked their opinion about the ideal grade organization for middle schools, only 3% favored the grades 7-9 junior high school plan. Sixty-five percent (65%) of the principals responding to this the survey believed that grades 6-8 middle school best served young adolescents (Valentine, Clark, Hackmann, & Petzko, 2002, p.12). Principals responding to the study were also asked their opinions about the most developmentally responsive district pattern. Sixty-two percent (62%) of all respondents indicated that K-5, 6-8, 9-12 was the best plan. An additional 14% favored the K-4, 5-8, 9-12 plan. The two district level plans respondents considered the least developmentally responsive were K-8, 9-12 (1%), and K-12 (0%) (p. 13).

The view that K-8 schools are considered one of the least appropriate grade organizations for the education of young adolescents is reflected in the decreasing number of these schools over the last several decades. For example, there were 5,552 Pre K/K-8 schools in 1988 and only 4,332 in 2001 (Alexander & McEwin, 1989; Market Data Retrieval, 2001). This trend may be surprising to some because of the highly publicized reorganization of several districts from middle schools to the K-8, 9-12 plan (Harrington-Lueker, 2001).

Conclusions

The vast majority of the school districts in the nation continue to organize schools into the three-tier organizational plan. The most common district organizational plan is grades K-5, 6-8, 9-12. This plan, along with the K-4, 5-8, and 9-12 plan, receives wide support from those responsible for the education of young adolescents. Significant decreases in the numbers of grades 7-9 junior high schools as well as less dramatic decreases in grades 7-8 middle school and the grades K-8 elementary school have occurred. The premise that young adolescents need and deserve a school devoted exclusively to their education and welfare is widely accepted by educators, policy makers, parents, and other stakeholders across the nation.

Recommendations

Grade organization decisions should be driven by the developmental characteristics, needs, and interests of young adolescents rather than by expediency. When possible, middle schools should house grades 5-8 or 6-8. These grade levels should be included because they are the grades in which young adolescents are typically enrolled. Placing these youth in schools that focus directly and exclusively on their needs and interests increases the chance that they will be more successful learners during a challenging time of their development.

Having young adolescents in a school designed exclusively for them allows all professionals at the school to focus directly and fully on providing the best learning opportunities possible. Educators in separately organized middle schools do not have to divide their energies between two or more developmental age groups (e.g., young children and young adolescents in grades K-8 elementary schools).

When separately organized middle schools are not possible, steps should be taken to establish "middle schools within schools" so that programs and practices that benefit young adolescents can be implemented to the fullest extent possible.

School Size

Heightened interest in the effects of school size (student enrollments) has emerged in recent years as proponents of small schools have become more vocal and increased research has been conducted that favors smaller schools. One problem with the research being conducted, however, is the lack of agreement among researchers about what size constitutes "small" and "large" student populations (Cotton, 1996; Williams, 1990). In other words, how small is small and how large is large? Where is the dividing line? According to many writers, however, large middle and high schools have become "a fact of life" in the nation (Allen, 2002, p. 36; Cotton, 1996).

Although research has not been able to firmly establish an ideal school enrollment size, some researchers have reported many benefits for smaller schools (Klonsky, 2002; Raywid, 2002; Shah, 2001). Others suggest that smaller schools maximize achievement in impoverished communities while larger schools maximize achievement among more affluent students (Howley, 1994). Proponents of smaller schools also believe that downsizing will lead to safer, more humane, and more effective schools that can reach a diversity of students more effectively (Klonsky, 2002; Raywid, 2002).

Authorities on middle school education also frequently support organizational arrangements that create a sense of smallness while permitting the development of long-term relationships between teachers and students and among students themselves (e.g., multiage grouping, looping, schools-within-a-school) (George & Lounsbury, 2000). In *Turning Points 2000,* Jackson and Davis recommend that middle schools not exceed 600 students (2002, p. 123). This belief seems to be supported by middle level principals. A national study of 1,423 principals conducted by Valentine and his associates found that 42% believed that the ideal middle school size was 400 to 599. Twenty-seven percent (27%) of the respondents selected an ideal size of between 600 and 799. Only 10% believed middle schools should exceed 800 students (Valentine, Clark, Hackmann, & Petzko, 2002, p.13). The opinions emerging from the *Turning Points* recommendations and opinions of middle school principals are rather closely aligned with the majority of research that indicates that 400-800 students is an ideal school size for both middle and high schools (Cotton, 1996; Williams, 1990).

Conclusions

When large is defined as 800 students or more, the percentage of large middle schools decreased 4% as compared to results from the 1993 study. This pattern is a reversal of the trend toward larger middle schools that occurred from the 1960s to the early 1990s. The trend toward fewer large middle schools was paralleled by a 3% increase in small middle schools that enroll 400 or fewer students. The percentage of middle schools with enrollments of between 401 and 800 remained virtually the same during this time period. Based on the results of this study, middle schools have not become larger during the intervening years between the 1993 and 2001 studies. About one-half of middle schools in the present study enrolled between 401 and 800 students. Additionally, approximately one-fourth had 400 or fewer students with the remaining one-fourth enrolling 800 or more students. Similar results were found by Valentine and his associates in a national survey of middle and junior high schools (2002, p. 137).

Recommendations

When possible, the school populations of middle schools should be kept in the 400 to 800 range. When larger schools are unavoidable, great care should be taken to establish "schools-within-a-school" plans to assure that young adolescents are not placed is schools that are impersonal and ineffective.

Team Organization

Interdisciplinary team organization is one of the success stories of the middle school movement (Arnold & Stevenson, 1998; Dickinson & Erb, 1997; Erb, 2001b). The importance of the team organization approach is widely acknowledged by both middle school authorities and middle level practitioners. For example, George and Alexander (2003) state, "the interdisciplinary team organization has been the most significant contribution of the middle school concept to the process of schooling" (p. 302).

Support for interdisciplinary team organization has grown stronger in recent years for multiple reasons not discussed here. However, one of the primary reasons for increasing numbers of middle schools implementing the team organization model is an expanding research base that documents a close correlation between team organization and student achievement as measured by standardized tests (Felner et al., 1997; Felner, Mertens, & Lipsitz, 1996; Flowers, Mertens, & Mulhall, 1999; McEwin, Greene, & Jenkins, 2001).

Research has also shown that interdisciplinary team organization must be accompanied by common planning time if teaming is going to be highly successful (Erb, 2001b; Flowers, Mertens & Mulhall, 1999, 2000). When schools provide high levels of common planning time, teachers more frequently integrate instruction and engage in other activities that increase student learning. Team size is also an important factor in the success of teaming. Although research has not determined what team size is optimal for the various grade levels, some recent studies have found that teams with 90 or fewer students are more successful in some ways than are larger teams (e.g., engaging in team level activities related to curriculum, assessment, and student assignments) (Flowers, Mertens, & Mulhall, 2000; Stevenson, 2002; Warren & Muth, 1995).

Conclusions

There has been significant growth in the percentage of the nation's middle schools utilizing the interdisciplinary team organization model (a 25% increase since the 1993 study). The most popular size for teams is four members with five being the next most popular team size. Two and three-teacher teams were found more frequently at the fifth and sixth grade levels. The most frequently reported number of common planning periods per week was five and ten, with each plan including about 40% of responding schools. Middle schools without common planning times were rare, but did exist (5%). Having team leaders was common practice in middle schools, with the most frequent selection process for these team leaders being appointment by the principal.

Recommendations

Interdisciplinary team organization should be utilized at all grade levels in all middle schools. All teachers on teams should be provided with daily common planning times and daily individual planning times. Team size should not exceed four teachers unless the fifth teacher is a resource teacher assigned to the team for special assistance to selected students (e.g., exceptional children's teachers). Whenever possible, teams at the fifth and sixth grade levels should be limited to two or three teachers.

Educators and other stakeholders should understand that interdisciplinary team organization alone does not guarantee success and should work diligently to take full advantage of the many positive effects teaming can have on student learning and healthy development.

Remedial Instruction Arrangements

Opportunities for remedial instruction are essential for young adolescents enrolled in middle schools. These opportunities are provided in a variety of forms and contexts. The ultimate goal of these programs, however, is to advance the knowledge and skills of individuals by providing them with focused instruction in their areas of difficulty.

Conclusions

Middle schools have increased the number and variety of remedial instruction arrangements available to young adolescents. The most significant increases fall in the areas of tutoring programs before and after school, adding an extra period, and Saturday classes. This increase in the provision of remedial activities is likely due, at least in part, to the powerful influences and pressures of high stakes testing.

Recommendations

Opportunities for remedial instruction are important to the success of many young adolescents and should be available in all middle schools. Instruction provided in these remedial activities should be of high quality and organized in ways that minimize the stigma sometimes associated with such instruction. The ultimate goal of these instructional opportunities should be to increase student learning in targeted areas so that the students involved can spend most of their instructional time learning with their peers. The overall goal of the instructional program of the school should be to continually improve learning opportunities for all young adolescents so that the need for remedial instruction is minimized.

Scheduling Plans

Flexible block scheduling is one of the key components of successful middle schools (George & Alexander, 2003; National Middle School Association, 1995). Flexible blocks of time are essential to allow teachers to group and regroup young adolescents for instruction and engage them in instructional activities that accommodate their individual learning needs. There are multiple reasons for creating flexible schedules that are well documented in the literature and not discussed here. A major reason, however, is that "these schedules give teachers the opportunity to make judgments about how much time should be given to each of the subjects under their jurisdiction, considering the characteristics of the students in their charge" (George & Alexander, 2003, p. 444).

Conclusions

Although the organization of school schedules utilizing uniform periods remains a popular practice, the use of this plan has decreased in grades six through eight. This trend reverses that of previous studies where steady increases were found. The most popular number of periods per day in schools using uniform periods was eight followed by six. Many of the schools reporting use of uniform periods also indicated that their schools utilized interdisciplinary team organization with common planning time for teachers. Therefore, it can be logically concluded that many schools utilizing uniform periods are combining several of these periods each day to form blocks of time allocated to the core subjects.

Recommendations

All middle schools should adopt some form of flexible block scheduling that provides teachers with multiple opportunities to make sound decisions regarding curriculum and instruction for the young adolescents they teach.

Time Allocated for Core Instruction

Instruction in the core subjects has always been a high priority in the nation's middle schools. One measure of the priority that core subjects have in middle schools is the allocation of time they receive in the school schedule. There is some concern that high stakes testing has influenced the priority given to "tested" and "non-tested" subject areas. For example, frequently tested subjects such as language arts may receive much larger portions of instructional time than subjects such as social studies that are less frequently tested. There is also concern among some critics of the middle school that the core subjects themselves are not receiving strong support or given a high priority.

Conclusions
Language arts receives the largest allocation of instructional time in middle schools with mathematics receiving the next largest number of minutes. Instructional time provided for science and social studies was not equal to mathematics and language arts. However, time differences were not substantial. It is possible that larger amounts of instructional time are provided for language arts because of the multiple components included in that subject area (e.g., writing, reading and speaking). It does not appear that high stakes testing has skewed the importance given the tested subjects, at least as measured by the amount of time allocated for instruction. Additionally, it is clear that middle schools have continued to allocate large portions of the instructional day to teaching the core subjects (e.g., three hours and 35 minutes at the seventh and eighth grade levels).

Recommendations
The strong emphasis on providing substantial portions of the school day for teaching the core subjects of language arts, science, mathematics, and social studies should continue. Although the four core subjects do not necessarily need equal amounts of time in the instructional day, care should be taken to make sure that both tested and non-tested subjects receive sufficient instructional time.

Required Non-Core Subjects

Middle schools typically require some subjects other than the core ones of language arts, social studies, mathematics, and science (Alexander & McEwin, 1989; Epstein & Mac Iver, 1990; McEwin, Dickinson, & Jenkins, 1996; Valentine, Clark, Hackmann, & Petzko, 2002). For example, in some middle schools, subjects such as music and visual arts are required of all middle school students, especially those enrolled in the lower middle grades. Other non-core subjects such as physical education and health may also be required of all students.

Conclusions
Required non-core subjects have changed little since the earlier studies. Physical education continued to be required in the overwhelming majority of middle schools. Health, reading, computers, and art were also popular choices. Sex education and general music were required at approximately one-fourth of schools at some grade levels.

Recommendations
Key subjects such as health, physical education, reading, and sex education should be required components of the middle school curriculum. These subjects do not have to be scheduled on a daily, year-long basis for all grade levels. However, the content of these subjects is too important to the education of young adolescents to be left to the chance that students might not elect to take them.

Elective Subjects

Middle schools typically offer a variety of elective subjects to enrich the learning of young adolescents. Popular offerings at the middle school level include subjects such as band, chorus, art, computers, and foreign languages. Students enrolled in the upper middle grades are frequently given opportunities to select several elective subjects with those in the lower grades having more required and fewer elective subjects from which to choose.

Conclusions
The range of elective subjects offered has changed little since the earlier studies. Band, orchestra, chorus, and art were among the most popular electives available to young adolescents. Other frequently offered electives

included computers, foreign language, industrial arts, and family and consumer science. Subjects such as general music and reading were more often offered as electives at the fifth and sixth grade levels. Subjects such as family and consumer science and industrial arts, traditionally offered in junior high schools and middle schools, have decreased in popularity.

Recommendations

A variety of elective courses should continue to be offered in middle schools. These elective courses should be carefully monitored to assure inclusion of all young adolescents. Decisions regarding what elective subjects should be offered, and which students enroll in those subjects, should be based on the needs and interests of young adolescents.

Interest Class/Mini-Course Programs

Providing opportunities for young adolescents to explore their interests and talents, and to encourage them to identify new interests and talents, have been identified as a goal of middle school education in both the junior high school and middle school movements (George & Alexander, 2003; Gruhn & Douglas, 1947). One of the ways many middle schools seek to reach this goal is through interest class/mini-course programs.

As standards-based reform influences more middle schools to base their curricula on state and national standards, the curriculum is becoming more standardized. George and Alexander (2003) noted: "As a result, students may find much of their experience less interesting, certainly less personally meaningful, or just plain dull" (p. 118). Perhaps this is one reason for the increasing numbers of middle schools offering these short term, student interest-centered courses.

Conclusions

Despite the many demands by subject areas and other programs and practices for a portion of the curriculum and school schedule, increasing percentages of middle schools were found to be providing mini-courses as an integral part of the curriculum. These mini-courses, defined in the survey instrument as short-term, student interest-centered courses, frequently focused on themes such as technology, fine arts, performing arts, academics, and personal development

Recommendations

Rich and varied interest class/mini-course programs should be an important part of the curriculum at all middle schools. These mini-courses should be carefully planned and offer all young adolescents multiple opportunities to explore their interests in ways that enrich their learning and contribute to their healthy personal development.

Teacher-Based Guidance (Advisory) Programs

The importance of teacher-based guidance programs has been recognized since the early days of the middle school movement (Alexander, Williams, Compton, Hines, & Prescott, 1968) and has its roots in the junior high school concept of "home room" (Briggs, 1920; Van Til, Vars, & Lounsbury, 1961). Although this important program has not been successfully implemented in many middle schools, it continues to be strongly advocated by middle school authorities as essential to the education and welfare of young adolescents (Burkhardt, 2001; Galassi, Gulledge, & Cox, 1998; George & Alexander, 2003; Jackson & Davis, 2000; Jenkins & Daniel, 2000; National Middle School Association, 1995).

Conclusions

The full and successful implementation of advisory periods in the nation's middle school remains an elusive goal. The percentage of schools with advisory programs increased from 39% to 47% between 1988 and 1993. However, an increase of only 1% occurred between the years of 1993 and 2001. This stagnation in the percentage of middle schools with advisory programs does not seem to be the result of principals' not believing these programs are important. For example, a recent national study of middle level principals found that 79% considered regularly scheduled adviser-advisee programs either important (31%) or very important (48%). Thirty-two percent (32%) of these principals reported that advisory programs were implemented in their schools with an additional 25% noting partial implementation (Valentine, Clark, Hackmann, & Petzko, 2002, p. 76).

In schools with advisory programs, the majority of teachers serve as advisors, with most advisory periods being scheduled for 16-30 minutes. Time allocated for advisory had increased since the 1993 study. However, the percentage of middle schools scheduling daily advisory periods decreased from 78% in 1988 to 56% in 2001.

Recommendations

Carefully planned teacher-based guidance (advisory) programs should be a component of all middle schools. Advisory should be scheduled on a daily basis for at least 25 minutes.

Comprehensive staff development should be provided for teacher advisors, guidance personnel, administrators, and other stakeholders responsible for the success of the program.

The advisory program should be accompanied by other advocacy efforts that fall outside the realm of scheduled advisory time, and curriculum for advisory programs should be carefully planned, articulated, and implemented.

Interschool Sports Programs

Competitive interschool sports programs continue to be very popular at middle schools across the nation despite decades of research that points out the dangers of contact sports for 10 to 14 year olds (Gerdy, 2000; McEwin & Dickinson, 1996, 1998). Other concerns regarding interschool sports competition for this developmental age group include: (a) emotional pressures placed on immature players by coaches, peers, parents, and community members; (b) high dropout rates caused by early and intense involvement; and, (c) unrealistic expectations by young adolescents and their parents about the possibility of receiving college scholarships and/or being selected by professional sports teams (McEwin & Dickinson, 1998). Despite these and other concerns, however, the popularity of organized, competitive sports has increased in recent years. This is due, at least in part, to the high level of importance given sports by American society.

Conclusions

The popularity of middle school competitive sports had reached a historic high with virtually all middle schools having competitive sports at one or more grade levels (96%). This percentage represents a 19% increase since 1993 and 46% increase since 1968. Opportunities for participating in sports increased in grades seven and eight as compared to grades five and six. The most frequently offered interschool sports for boys were basketball, track, wrestling, and soccer. Sports most often offered for girls were basketball, track, volleyball, cross country, and softball. These sports were also among the most popular during the earlier studies.

The sports most often added were soccer, softball, volleyball, cross country, wrestling, and track. Although specific information regarding intramural sports was not collected in the study, another recent national study found that the percentage of middle schools offering intramural programs decreased in recent years (Valentine, Clark, Hackmann, & Petzko, 2002). This finding is consistent with results of the 1988 and 1993 studies. In summary, middle schools have moved dramatically in the direction of adding interschool sports programs and dropping intramural sports programs. These trends are alarming and need and deserve the immediate attention of middle school educators, policy makers, and other responsible stakeholders. It is of particular concern that young adolescents in many middle schools who are not playing on varsity teams have no opportunity to participate or benefit from sports participation of any type.

Recommendations

When interschool sports are offered at middle schools, the specific sports included and decisions about which age groups are permitted to participate should be carefully considered and carried out. All coaches should be knowledgeable about the developmental period of early adolescence and make decisions based on that knowledge. Steps should also be taken to make sure that sports equipment fits properly and that playing fields are safe and well maintained. Interschool sports should be open to all young adolescents, not just those who have developed physically at an early age.

Intramural sports programs that are inclusive and carefully planned should be an important part of all middle school sports programs.

Interdisciplinary Instruction and Instructional Strategies

Middle school literature, and to some extent later junior high school literature, has continually included advocacy for curriculum and instruction that is not only interdisciplinary, but also integrative (Beane, 1993, 1997; Eichhorn, 1966; Lounsbury & Vars, 1978; National Middle School Association, 2002; Van Til, Vars, & Lounsbury, 1961). However, the decades-long struggle to move away from subject-centered curriculum and instruction to more integrative models has met with only limited success.

Conclusions

As compared with results from the 1993 study, a smaller percentage of respondents estimated that interdisciplinary instruction was utilized in their schools only 1 to 20 percent of the instructional day. Other trends regarding the amount of time devoted to interdisciplinary instruction revealed some positive increases. However, the increases were not dramatic. Clearly, much remains to be accomplished in the nation's middle schools if curriculum and instruction is to become truly integrative.

As was the case in the 1993 study, the most frequently used instructional strategy reported was direct instruction. However, as noted earlier, an increase in the use of cooperative learning on a regular basis increased by an average of 10%. Increases in the use of independent study on a regular basis were also reported, especially at the fifth and sixth grade levels.

Recommendations

The authors agree with the NMSA position that the developmental and learning characteristics of young adolescents should provide the foundation for selecting teaching strategies and that these strategies should "enhance and accommodate the diverse skills, abilities, and knowledge of young adolescents, cultivate multiple intelligences, and capitalize on students' individual learning styles" (National Middle School Association, 1995, p. 24). One of the best ways to provide the kind of instruction that best meets the needs and interests of young adolescents is to make that instruction integrative and inclusive of the subjects students study at the middle school level. Providing curriculum and instruction that is integrative should be a major goal of all middle schools.

Instructional Grouping Practices

As has been the case for decades, the best way to group young adolescents for instruction continues to be a controversial issue. Proponents of tracking – a layering of an age group of students into separate classes based on factors such as perceived ability or past achievement – support it based on the need to differentiate curriculum and instruction to provide beneficial effects for highly gifted students in accelerated classes. They also argue that "without ability grouping, the children who are at the top of their respective classes are generally given the least attention" (Gallagher, 1993, p. 9). However, as noted by George and Alexander (2003), "The great preponderance of the evidence weighs against tracking, while the great majority of school districts utilize it comprehensively" (p. 413). This is the case despite a comprehensive research base that shows tracking does not deliver the benefits claimed by proponents (e.g., increased academic achievement, positive social or personal effects) and that students are frequently grouped so that income, social class, and race are highly correlated with their placement levels (Gamoran & Berends, 1987; Gamoran & Weinstein, 1998; George & Alexander, 2003; George, Renzulli, & Reis, 1997; Good & Brophy, 2000; Oakes, 1985, 1995; Wheelock, 1992, 1998).

Conclusions

Ability grouping in the form of tracking is common practice in over three-fourths of middle schools (78%). When asked to select the one statement that best described their school's operating policy regarding instructional grouping, only 22% selected random grouping (no ability grouping). Results clearly show that the number of schools utilizing tracking practices in one or more of the core subjects has increased since the 1993 study. The most common forms of tracking utilized in responding middle schools were "all grades – certain subjects" and "certain grades – certain subjects." Tracking was most frequently utilized in mathematics, language arts, and reading. Only about one in ten middle schools reported tracking being used for social studies instruction.

Recommendations

The authors support the position taken by the National Forum to Accelerate Middle-Grades Reform that heterogeneous assignment of students should be the norm in all middle schools (2001). Educators and other stakeholders should "deliberately work to reduce disparities in educational attainment by adopting open and fair student assignment practices." When students are grouped and regrouped for instruction, the assignment should be "temporary and based on diagnosed needs, interests, and talents of students, not on a single achievement test" (p. 1). Instructional grouping practices should be based on the research base rather than on tradition. Furthermore, decisions about how to reduce or eliminate tracking should be accompanied by a comprehensive plan about what is going to replace the often-ingrained system. Simply mixing all students together for instruction without carefully articulated instructional strategies does not guarantee improved student learning. Reorganization plans must be comprehensive and accompanied by intensive and continuing professional development if high rates of success are to be achieved.

Student Progress Reports

There have been calls for improvement in the area of reporting student progress in the middle school literature for many years (National Middle School Association 1995; Vars, 1992, 2001). *This We Believe* (National Middle School Association, 1995) states, "Middle level students need to participate in all phases of assessment and evaluation, helping to set individual and group goals, identifying ways to measure progress, and evaluating their own accomplishments" (pp. 26-27). This approach seems to be contrary to the current emphasis in many middle schools on conventional competitive assessments, evaluation, and marking (Vars, 2001).

Conclusions

Although respondents described a wide variety of student progress reporting mechanisms, the most popular method remained the traditional letter scale. This result mirrors findings of the 1968, 1988, and 1993 studies. Parent conferences and informal notes were also utilized in the majority of all middle schools. Percentage marks and S/U scales were used in about four of ten middle schools. Some increase was found in the use of portfolios

Recommendations

A variety of methods for reporting student progress should be utilized by all middle schools. Care should be taken to be sure that student progress reporting goes beyond "letter grades" that compare student learning with the progress, or lack thereof, of other students. As recommended by National Middle School Association (1995), ". . . assessment and evaluation should emphasize individual progress rather than comparison with other students" (p. 27). One effective approach to making student progress reporting more individualized is through the use of student portfolios.

Faculty

A primary barrier to the full success of middle schools has been a continued lack of teachers who wish to teach at the middle level and who have the specialized professional preparation to do so expertly. This lack of specially prepared middle level teachers has resulted in many thousands of young adolescents being taught by teachers who, at least initially, do not have the specialized knowledge, skills, and dispositions needed to be highly successful (Dickinson, 2001; McEwin & Dickinson, 1995; McEwin, Dickinson, Erb, &

Scales, 1995; McEwin, Dickinson, & Smith, 2002, 2003). The future success of middle schools lies, at least in part, on remedying this unfortunate situation. Young adolescents need and deserve teachers who want to teach them and have the specialized professional preparation necessary to do so successfully.

Conclusions

Progress has been made in the percentage of schools reporting higher levels of teachers who have specialized professional preparation to teach at the middle level. Although this progress was not dramatic, trends moved in a positive direction. Results from the current study also found that increasing percentages of middle level teachers find teaching young adolescents satisfying and are not seeking transfers to elementary or senior high schools.

Recommendations

Middle school practitioners should work collaboratively with policy makers, teacher preparation representatives, state department of education officials, professional practice board members, and other stakeholders to create specialized middle level teacher preparation programs and the mandatory licensure regulations that assure that all teachers of young adolescents have the specialized knowledge, skills, and dispositions needed to be successful. In states where these specialized programs and licensure regulations already exist, steps should be taken to ensure that these gains are not lost in the name of administrative convenience (e.g., difficulty of finding teachers in a time of teacher shortage).

Graduate programs that provide practicing middle level teachers with opportunities to enrich their knowledge and skills should also be universally available. Knowing that many middle school teachers will continue to enter their practice without specialized middle level professional preparation, it is also essential that high-quality, ongoing professional development activities be available in all middle schools.

High Stakes Testing

One of the more recent conditions that middle school educators find themselves dealing with that was not the case in many states when the 1968, 1988, and 1993 studies were conducted is the reality of high stakes accountability systems. While accountability systems have been present in schools and school districts for many years, the idea of placing significant consequences to the results of accountability-based testing is of recent origin. Most of these accountability systems had their genesis in the mid-1990s.

The target of high stakes accountability systems is the individual school, as contrasted to earlier accountability measures where the unit of accountability was the school district. In accountability models utilizing high stakes standardized testing, schools are typically given pre-determined targets as expectations for student performance. Generally, these targets are expectations of growth from previous levels of performance. Additionally, most high stakes testing systems have positive and negative consequences that are placed on individual schools based on high stakes test results. In the lowest performing schools, these consequences may include removal of the principal, re-constitution of the school with all teachers and administrators being required to reapply for their positions, or the takeover of a school by the state.

The potential impact of high stakes testing on middle school programs and practices caused the researchers to create two survey items addressing the effect of high stakes testing on middle school programs and practices. A brief discussion of the results of these survey items is presented below.

Conclusions

The majority of respondents indicated that high stakes testing had no effect on advisory programs at their schools. About one-fourth believed the effect was positive with only about 15% reporting a negative effect. This result is interesting due to widespread anecdotal information about advisory times being devoted predominately to test preparation in many middle schools.

The influence of high stakes testing on curriculum was more pronounced with only 6% indicating that there had been no effect. It was somewhat surprising to the authors that over eight of every ten respondents believed that high stakes testing affected curriculum positively, with only 14% noting negative effects. This finding is interesting considering many critics of high stakes testing contend that it narrows the curriculum at the expense of other important "non-core" and "non-academic" programs such as elective courses, advisory programs, and co-curricular programs and activities. Results seem to indicate that high stakes testing has, at least to some extent, resulted in a more intense focus on curriculum. However, when results from other parts of the study are considered, it seems possible that some of this increased focus on the core curriculum may have come at the expense of time and effort formerly placed on other components of the school curriculum, for example, elective courses.

Results of the effects of high stakes testing on elective subjects revealed that approximately one-third of respondents felt that there had been no effect.

The remaining two-thirds were almost evenly divided on whether the effect had been positive or negative. Although respondents were not asked to explain their responses, it seems that the renewed focus on subjects typically tested in high stakes assessments may have received increased emphasis at the expense of that previously provided as elective subjects.

Almost three-fourths of respondents perceived that high stakes testing had positive effects on instruction at their schools, with only 17% noting a negative impact. Based on the limited data regarding instruction included in this study, there does not seem to have been a movement away from effective instructional strategies. The overall result, at least in the views of the respondents, of high stakes testing has been improved instruction.

The majority of respondents also believed that high stakes testing had positive effects on instructional grouping plans. As was the case with instruction, 17% viewed the impact as negative. Perhaps high stakes testing has helped re-focus instructional grouping around student performance levels, with those students who need it receiving more time and attention. One danger that exists, however, is the possibility that high stakes testing is being used as a rationale to move increasingly to rigid tracking practices.

More than eight in ten respondents felt that the impact of high stakes testing on remediation was positive. It seems that high stakes testing has paved the way for more attention and effort being placed on remediation. As noted earlier in this section, these remediation activities come in a great variety of formats.

Responses regarding high stakes testing and scheduling resulted in a rather dispersed profile of responses. Approximately one-third perceived no impact, while 42% reported a positive influence and 22% a negative one. Although respondents were not asked why they felt the way they did, it seems logical that the majority believed that time has been reallocated because of the effects of high stakes testing. There does not seem to be a consensus, however, on whether these changes have helped or hindered the effectiveness of the schools involved.

About four in ten respondents believed that high stakes testing had resulted in negative impact on school climate. However, a similar percentage reported that the impact was positive. Perhaps a contributing factor to the negative responses is the pressure of trying to ensure that all young adolescents make high scores on standardized tests. This stress associated with this pressure would also likely carry over to the students themselves. On the positive impact side, one might speculate that since the majority of respondents see high stakes testing as positive, they might also feel that the overall results on school climate are positive.

Student learning is certainly at the core of what high stakes testing is purported to be about. Almost three-fourths of respondents indicated that the impact was positive. Clearly, they believe that high stakes testing has focused the attention of schools more intensely on student learning. Only 16% viewed the impact as negative, while 10% did not believe student learning had been impacted.

Approximately one-third of respondents reported that high stakes testing had no effect on teacher planning time, while 41% viewed the effect as positive and one-fourth as negative. Respondents were not asked to explain the rationale for their choices. However, it is possible that teachers of core subjects, especially the tested ones, received more time for planning than they did before high stakes testing. It is also reasonable, however, to suggest that in some schools teacher planning time may have been reduced to provide more time for instruction.

While over one-third of respondents reported that high stakes testing had no effect of teaming at their schools, one-half felt the impact had been positive and 17% negative. The reasons for choices made by respondents are not known. One might speculate, however, that positive results stemmed from the increased incidence of teaming in responding middle schools and the provision of increased time for teacher planning. It is also possible that factors such as the reduction or loss of common planning time and the increased use of tracking have caused some respondents to report a negative impact of high stakes testing on teaming at their schools.

As noted earlier, respondents were also asked to indicate how high stakes testing had affected the use of time in their schools. Results revealed that three-fourths of respondents reported an increased use of time for remediation. Additionally, over one-half reported increased time being provided for instruction. One-third indicated that less time was being provided for elective subjects. Small percentages also noted reduced time being provided for advisory programs, teacher planning, instruction, and remediation.

The majority of respondents in the current study believed that high stakes testing had positively impacted programs and practices at their schools in five of eleven categories. In the other six categories, 27% to 48% of the respondents showed a similar belief in the positive impact of high stakes testing. These findings are similar to results of a national study of middle level principals conducted by Valentine and his associates (2002, pp. 99-100). This should not, however, be perceived as a blanket endorsement for high stakes testing by respondents of this study. As shown in Table 30, a significant percentage of those completing the survey believed that high stakes testing had no impact on the programs and practices at their schools (approximately 25%). Also, from

8% to 41% of those completing the survey reported negative impacts at their schools. The highest levels of concern included important components such as school climate, electives, and teacher planning time.

Recommendations

Great care should be taken by middle school educators, policymakers, and others responsible for the education and welfare of young adolescents to ensure that middle schools are standards-driven rather than test-driven. Schools that place too much emphasis on student scores derived from high stakes standardized tests administered once a year run the risk of focusing intensely on rote learning at the expense of more authentic learning.

The authors agree with the National Forum to Accelerate Middle Grades Reform (2002): "no single test should ever be the sole determinant of a young adolescent's future, whether it be promotion to the next grade, special placement, or transition from the middle grades to high school." Rather the emphasis should be placed on standards and assessments that "lead to high expectations, foster high quality instruction, and support higher levels of learning for every student" (p. 1). The trap of believing that the implementation of high stakes testing programs alone leads to high achieving middle schools where all young adolescents receive the quality education program they need and deserve should be avoided.

Results of standardized tests should be only one of the many tools used to help all young adolescents reach their full potentials. Emphasis should be placed on authentic assessments such as portfolios, exhibitions, performances, and demonstrations. Multiple assessments that are an integral part of curriculum and instruction should be utilized and flow from what is being taught. Assessment should be learner-centered and include self-assessments, peer assessments, journals, logs, products, and other effective strategies (Donald, 1997).

Concluding Statements

As noted by one of the authors of this study, "There is nothing wrong with the middle school concept. The concept – a school for young adolescents based on their developmental needs – is as valid today as it was in either of its previous iterations at the turn of the 20th century or in the early 1960s....It is a flexible, responsive, integrated concept with the aim of providing a safe, secure, and appropriate environment for a young adolescent to learn challenging content that will enable him or her to explore self, others, and the larger world" (Dickinson, 2001, p. 1).

Unfortunately, however, many middle schools have not progressed beyond the initial stages of reorganizing and adding selected components commonly associated with the middle school concept. For example, they may have implemented an interdisciplinary team organization model, but not be utilizing that model in ways that lead to high levels of student learning and healthy development. Too many middle schools have reached a stage that Dickinson calls "arrested development"; the middle school concept has not been completely implemented or it was once successfully implemented, but has grown static and unresponsive (Dickinson, 2001, p. 4).

Being aware of this situation, the researchers conducted the present study, at least in part, to determine if the nation's middle schools have continued to progress toward programs and practices that reflect the middle school concept, have stalled in a stage of "arrested development," or retreated from the model using high stakes testing or other trends as excuses for not moving forward. As the readers will recognize as they examine the results of this study, the news is both good and bad. For example, progress has been made in the implementation of interdisciplinary team organization to the point where 77% of schools have implemented the model. This represents a 25% increase since the 1993 study. One wonders, however, why all middle schools have not implemented this signature practice that has proven so successful at increasing student learning when implemented appropriately.

In addition to interdisciplinary team organization, areas where progress has been made – as measured by percentages of schools reporting implementation of the program or practice – include: (a) the increased use of cooperative learning and other appropriate instructional strategies; (b) increased availability of remedial instruction opportunities; (c) significant amounts of time being allotted for instruction in core subjects; (d) wider implementation of interest/mini-class programs; (e) increased use of interdisciplinary instruction; (f) continued offering of appropriate required subjects as well as a variety of elective courses; and, (g) larger percentages of schools employing teachers who have specialized professional preparation to teach young adolescents.

A lack of substantial progress was found in the areas of: (a) implementation of teacher-based guidance (advisory) programs: (b) a dramatic increase in interschool sports programs including those sports that are especially dangerous for young adolescents; (c) continued strong dependence on direct instruction as a primary teaching strategy; and, (d) increased use of tracking as an instructional grouping practice. The reader should understand that the lists just provided are general representational findings of the study. More detailed information, including results not mentioned here, is found in the body of this report (e.g., student progress reporting, listing of required courses). Figures, summaries of findings by topic, conclusions made by the researchers, and recommendations for action are also included.

How Fares the American Middle School?

Is the decades' long movement to create schools that focus directly and exclusively on the developmental realities of young adolescents yet another failed attempt to effect authentic, meaningful, and positive change to the traditions of American education? Is the middle school destined to become more like the typical subject-centered, depersonalized senior high school as did its unsuccessful predecessor, the junior high school? Is the middle school doomed to its present level of arrested development? This study does not provide full answers to these and other important questions. However, it does offer clues regarding the progress, made, or lack thereof, and provides readers with data that may be useful in their attempts to improve programs and practices at their schools.

The researchers were both heartened by progress made in areas such as interdisciplinary team organization and the specialized middle level professional preparation and concerned by the lack of progress made in the implementation of teacher-based guidance programs. An additional cause for concern was the growing use of tracking as an instructional method in increasing percentages of middle schools.

The authors do, however, believe that the American middle school continues to be the best place to educate young adolescents. Moving them to an elementary school designed for young children (e.g., grades K-8) or a senior-high school designed for older adolescents (e.g., grades 7-12) only further compounds the difficult, complex, and crucial task of designing and implementing middle school programs and practices that truly reflect what is known about the most effective ways to provide high quality learning experiences for young adolescents. As noted earlier, there is nothing wrong with the middle school concept. What is required is courageous, deliberate, collaborative efforts by all those responsible for the education and welfare of the age group to create authentic middle schools that are reflective of what those schools should and could be. Half-measures lead only to partial implementation and result in limited success.

The kind of concerted action needed must be put forth in spite of federal legislation that operates on the false belief that all that is needed to guarantee that all students learn at high levels is to hold schools and educators accountable through the use of high stakes standardized tests and punitive measures. Fortunately, young adolescents who are enrolled in middle schools that have faithfully followed the middle school model score the highest on high stakes standardized tests (Felner et al., 1997; Felner, Mertens, & Lipsitz, 1996; Lee & Smith, 1993; McEwin, Greene, & Jenkins, 2001). Unfortunately, many educators and policymakers seem unaware of this research base or choose to ignore it because it does not support their beliefs or causes.

There are many reasons why the middle school concept must be more comprehensively applied in middle schools as well as in other school organizations that house young adolescents. The most important reason is that the education and welfare of young adolescents is at stake. We know what to do and how to do it. There are excellent middle schools in every state that can serve as reform models. There is a growing research base that supports the middle school model. It is time for all of us to work diligently and collaboratively toward the goal of making sure that all young adolescents have the opportunities that are provided by high quality middle schools that best reflect what is known. Ignoring this responsibility can only result in young adolescents failing to reach their full potentials as individuals and productive citizens.◆

References

Alexander, W. M. (1968). *A survey of organizational patterns of reorganized middle schools.* Washington, DC: United States Department of Health, Education, and Welfare.

Alexander, W. M., & McEwin, C. K. (1989). *Schools in the middle: Status and progress.* Columbus, OH: National Middle School Association.

Alexander, W. M., Williams, E., Compton, M., Hines, V., & Prescott, D. (1968). *The emergent middle school.* New York: Holt, Rinehart and Winston.

Allen, R. (2002). Big schools: The way we are. *Educational Leadership, 59* (5), 36-37.

Arnold, J., & Stevenson, C. (1998). *Teacher's teaming handbook: A middle level planning guide.* Fort Worth, TX: Harcourt Brace.

Beane, J. A. (1993). *A middle school curriculum: From rhetoric to reality* (2nd ed.). Columbus, OH: National Middle School Association.

Beane, J. A. (1997). *Curriculum integration: Designing the core of democratic education.* New York: Teachers College Press.

Briggs, T. H. (1920). *The junior high school.* Boston: Houghton Mifflin Company.

Burkhardt, R. M. (2001). Advisory: Advocacy for every student. In T. O. Erb (Ed.). *This we believe...and now we must act* (pp. 35-41). Westerville, OH: National Middle School Association.

Cotton, K. (1996). *School size, school climate, and student performance.* Portland, OR: Northwest Regional Educational Laboratory.

Dickinson, T. S. (Ed.). (2001). *Reinventing the middle school.* New York: Routledge Falmer.

Dickinson, T. S., & Erb, T. O. (1997). *We gain more than we give: Teaming in middle schools.* Columbus, OH: National Middle School Association.

Donald, J. (1997). *Improving the environment for learning.* San Francisco: Jossey-Bass Publishers.

Eichhorn, D. H. (1966). *The middle school.* New York: The Center for Applied Education.

Erb. T. O. (Ed.). (2001a). *This we believe...and now we must act.* Westerville, OH: National Middle School Association.

Erb, T.O. (2001b). Transforming organizational structures for young adolescents and adult learning. In T. S. Dickinson (Ed.), (pp. 176-200). *Reinventing the middle school.* New York: Routledge Falmer.

Epstein, J. L., & Mac Iver, D. J. (1990). *Education in the middle grades: National practices and trends.* Columbus, OH: National Middle School Association.

Felner. R. D., Jackson, A. W., Kasak, D., Mulhall, P., Brand, S., & Flowers, N. (1997). The impact of school reform for the middle years: Longitudinal study of a network engaged in Turning Points-based comprehensive school transformation. *Phi Delta Kappan, 78,* 528-532, 541-550.

Felner, J. L., Mertens, S., & Lipsitz, J. (1996). *Assessment of middle grades education in Michigan: A report of the W. K. Kellogg Foundation's Middle Start Initiative.* Urbana, IL: University of Illinois.

Flowers, N., Mertens, S. B., & Mulhall, P. F. (1999). The impact of teaming: Five research-based outcomes of teaming. *Middle School Journal, 31* (2), 57-60.

Flowers, N., Mertens, S. B., & Mulhall, P. F. (2000). How teaming influences classroom practices. *Middle School Journal, 32* (2), 52-59.

Galassi, J. P., Gulledge, S. A., & Cox, N. D. (1998). *Advisory: Definitions, descriptions, decisions, directions.* Columbus, OH: National Middle School Association.

Gallagher, J. J. (1993). *Ability grouping: A tool for educational excellence.* The College Board Review, No. 168.

Gamoran, A., & Berends, M. (1987). The effect of stratification in secondary schools: Synthesis of survey and ethnographic research. *Review of Educational Research, 57* (4), 415-435.

Gamoran, A., & Weinstein, M. (1998). Differentiation and opportunity in restructured schools. *American Journal of Education, 106* (3), 385-431.

George, P. S., & Alexander, W. M. (2003). *The exemplary middle school* (3rd ed.). Belmont, CA: Wadsworth/Thomas Learning.

George, P. S., & Lounsbury, J. H. (2000). *Making big schools feel small: Multiage grouping, looping, and schools-within-a-school.* Westerville, OH: National Middle School Association.

George, P. S., Renzulli, J., & Reis, S. (1997). *Dilemmas in talent development: Two views.* Columbus, OH: National Middle School Association.

Gerdy, J. R. (2000). *Sports in school: The future of an institution.* New York: Teachers College Press.

Good, T., & Brophy, J. (2000). *Looking in classrooms* (8th ed.). New York: Bantam Books.

Gruhn, W. T., & Douglas, H. R. (1947). *The modern junior high school.* New York: Ronald Press.

Harrington-Lueker, D. (2001, March 15). Middle schools fail to make the grade. *USA Today.*

Howley, C. (1994). *The academic effectiveness of small-scale schooling (An update).* ERIC Digest. Charleston, WV: Clearinghouse on Rural Education and Small Schools. (ED372 897)

Jackson, A. W., & Davis, G. A. (2002). *Turning points 2000: Educating adolescents in the 21st century*. New York: Teachers College Press.

Jenkins, J. M., & Daniel, B. S. (2000). *Banishing anonymity: Middle and high school advisement programs*. Larchmont, NY: Eye On Education.

Klonsky, M. (2002). How smaller schools prevent school violence. *Educational Leadership, 59* (5), 65-69.

Lee, V., & Smith, J. (1993). Effects of school restructuring on the achievement and engagement of middle grade students. *Sociology of Education, 66,* 164-187.

Lounsbury, J. H., & Vars, G. F. (1978). *A curriculum for the middle school years*. New York: Harper & Row, Publishers.

Market Data Retrieval (2001). Shelton, Connecticut.

McEwin, C. K., & Dickinson, T. S. (1996). Placing young adolescents at risk in interscholastic sports programs. *Clearing House, 73,* 211-213.

McEwin, C. K., & Dickinson, T. S. (1998). What role for middle school sports? *The School Administrator, 10,* 52-55.

McEwin, C. K., Dickinson, T. S., Erb, T., & Scales, P. C. (1995). *A vision of excellence: Organizing principles for middle grades teacher preparation*. Columbus, OH: National Middle School Association.

McEwin, C. K., Dickinson, T. S., & Jenkins D. M. (1996). *America's middle schools: Practices and progress – A twenty-five year perspective*. Columbus, OH: National Middle School Association.

McEwin, C. K., Dickinson, T. S., & Smith T. W. (2002). May I see your license please? *Principal Leadership 3* (1), 40-44.

McEwin, C. K., Dickinson, T. S., & Smith T. W. (2003). Why specialized preparation is critical. *Kappa Delta Pi Record 39* (2), 58-61.

McEwin, C. K., Greene, M. W., & Jenkins, D. M. (2001). *Where do North Carolina middle schools stand in the 21st century? A status report on programs and practices*. Pinehurst, NC: North Carolina Middle School Association.

National Forum to Accelerate Middle Grades Reform (2001). *National Forum policy statement: Student assignment in the middle grades: Towards academic success for all students*. Newton, MA: Author.

National Middle School Association (2002). *NMSA position paper on curriculum integration*. Westerville, OH: Author.

National Middle School Association (1995). *This we believe: Developmentally responsive middle level schools*. Columbus, OH: Author.

Oakes, J. (1985). *Keeping track: How schools structure inequality*. New Haven, CT: Yale University Press.

Oakes, J. (1995). More than meets the eye: Links between tracking and the culture of schools. In H. Pool & J. A. Page (Eds.), *Beyond tracking: Finding success in inclusive schools* (pp. 59-68). Bloomington, IN: Phi Delta Kappa Educational Foundation.

Raywid, M. A. (2002). The policy environments of small schools and schools-within-schools. *Educational Leadership, 59* (5), 47-51.

Shah. A. (2001, September 10). Smaller schools, bigger payoff? *The Star Tribune*, p. 1A.

Stevenson, C. (2002). *Teaching ten to fourteen year olds* (3rd ed). Boston: Allyn and Bacon.

Valentine, J. W., Clark, D. C., Hackmann, D. G., & Petzko, V. N. (2002). *A national study of leadership in middle level schools: Volume I: A national study of middle level leaders and school programs.* Reston, VA: National Association of Secondary School Principals.

Van Til, W., Vars, G. F., & Lounsbury, J. H. (1961). *Modern education for the junior high school years*. New York: The Bobbs-Merrill Company.

Vars, G. F. (1992). Humanizing student evaluation and reporting. In J. R. Irvin (Ed.), *Transforming middle level education* (pp. 336-365). Boston: Allyn and Bacon.

Vars, G. F. (2001). Assessment and evaluation that promote learning. In T. O. Erb (Ed.), *This we believe...and now we must act* (pp. 78-89). Westerville, OH: National Middle School Association.

Warren, L. L., & Muth, K. D. (1995). The impact of common planning time on middle grades students and teachers. *Research in Middle Level Education, 18* (3), 41-58.

Wheelock, A. (1992). *Crossing the tracks*. New York: New Press.

Wheelock, A. (1998). *Safe to be smart: Building a culture for standards-based reform in the middle grades*. Columbus, OH: National Middle School Association.

Williams, D. T. (1990). *The dimensions of education: Recent research on school size*. Working Paper Series. Clemson, SC: Clemson University. (ED 347 006)